What I Believe-Truth

Original Copyright- 2018
Updated Copyright- 2019

Bruce D. Durst

In cooperation with
Cyber Writers Gallery
ISBN 978-0-578-62383-2

Contents
What I Believe-Truth

Introduction...page 7

Chapter 1. Changing Times Long-Awaited Predictions for the Dawning Age...page 19
  A. New Age/New Thought religion...page 19
  B. Christian Science...page 20
  C. Science of Mind...page 20
  D. *Mind Power*...page 21

Chapter 2. In the Beginning...page 24
  A. Lemuria, a land forgotten...page 24
  B. Atlantis...page 28

Chapter 3 Nature's Intelligence...page 39
  A. Intuition...page 39
  B. *Mind Power* - **William W. Atkinson**...page 40
  C. Animal migration...page 43
  D. The Universal Mind...page 44
  E. **Jeremy Narby-*Intelligence In Nature***...page 44
    1. Intelligence in plants...page 44
    2. Intelligence in birds...page 49
    3. Intelligence in ants...page 53

4. Mankind has forgotten
the stars...page 56

Chapter 4 Conversing with The Universal
Mind…...page 59
A. Comprehension of messages from
Beyond...page 59

Chapter 5 The Law of Attraction…page 64
A. **Napoleon Hill-** *Think and Grow Rich* - A
something Within…page 64
B. The *Holy Bible*…page 65 and
The Law of Attraction...page 65
C. **Napoleon Hill-** *The Law of Success*,
The principles of achieving
success...page 66
D. **Deepak Chopra-** *The Seven Spiritual
Laws of Success*…page 67
E. Twelve principles of success by the
author of this writing…page 68
F. Visualize and Affirm...page 69
G. **Florence Scoville Shinn-** *The Game of
Life And How to Play it*…page 69
H. Messages of encouragement from
Rhonda Byrnes
The Secret...page 73
I. **Dr. Wayne Dyer -** *The Power of
Intention*…page 75
J. **Wallace D. Wattles -** *The Science of*

Getting Rich, there is a thinking
Stuff etc...page 77
K. Jack Canfield- *Key to Living The Law of Attraction*...page 81
L. **Michael Jeffreys- *Success Secrets of The Motivational Superstars*...page 84**

Chapter 6 Esoteric...page 97
A. Psychics, clairvoyants, palm readers and charlatans...page 97
B. **Annie Besant, Charles Leadbeater –** *Thought Forms,* Thoughts are things...page 99
C. Life before Birth – Reincarnation ...page 99
D. **Sylvia Browne-** *The Other Side and Back*...page 102. *Life After Life*...102 *On The Other Side*...page 102
E. **Ruth Montgomery-** *The World to Come –The Guides the Long-Awaited Predictions for the Dawning Age*...page 107
F. **Madame Blavatsky-** *The Secret Doctrine*...page108
G. **Ken Carey -** *The Third Millennium - Living In The Post–Historic World*...page 108
H. **Ruth Montgomery –** *Strangers*

Among Us-Walkins…page 113

I. **Ruth Montgomery - *Companions Along the Way***…page 119, **Dale Palmer-*The Esoteric Traditions*** …page 118-120

J. Rosicrucian writing…page 11

K. The education of **Master Jesus** …page 121

L. **Ken Carey – *Starseed Transmissions***…page 124

M. **Jeremy Narby - *Intelligence In Nature*.** Searching the Peruvian Amazon jungle with Shaman…page 127

N. **Ruth Montgomery-*The World To Come***…page 132

Appendix A- Recommended Reading

Notes

What I Believe-Truth
Introduction

Truth, what is truth? Are you seeking truth but, not receiving the answers, you want. Are you questioning the doctrine of your church? Many of the answers of the churches of today only lead to more questions. Truth is what you believe and the writings in this book and the authors presented here will lead you to the truth you are looking for.

In this volume, and the Recommended Authors and Writings section, there are more than sixty books. I have read the majority of these, and some, more than once. Some writers will speak of God others will not. But still all authors write Truth. If you want writings more directly from God then you need to read the books of Robert Collier and Neville Goddard. For more writings of truth directed more in the terms of Mother Nature, you can follow those authors in the book "The Secret" by Rhonda Byrne. In these writings I do not present any new or original ideas. All of these writings come from the ideas and content of the books I have read. Some of these writings may be more than 100,000 years old. Even the book "The Secret" written by Rhonda Byrne originated from the book "The Secret Of The Ages" written by Robert Collier, 1885 to 1950. The journey to truth can be a wonderful experience.

Copyright 2019 Introduction continued;

There was a time in my life when I started questioning the traditional teachings of the churches. So, I started studying more than just what was taught by the major religions. I said to myself, there has to be more to life than what they are teaching. I have a very logical mind, which I have developed through working on mechanical systems, electronics, computer systems, and mathematics. So, when I thought logically, it did not make sense that all the major religions were teaching; you have to go through the church to get to heaven. You have to be good through all your life for if you are bad you will be punished, when you die, by spending eternity in hell. This theory did not make sense to me, that a superior benevolent creator would punish us with eternal damnation. Then, I discovered an advertisement in the newspaper for a psychic fair. I had never heard of such a thing and decided I would try it. I found a group of people with strong psychic abilities at a church called Temple of the Living God in St. Petersburg Florida. Through my church visits and further self-study, I learned that we humans have an aura about us. This aura is within what we might call our personal space and contains colors of our moods and our life experiences called the Akashic records. Our aura and the Akashic records are supposed to contain the complete information of all our past lives. Some people have the ability to see auras. I do not. It was the beginning of my search for;

Truth. I started reading many books and found several that really caught my attention, these were written by members of the Theosophical society, namely, Helena P. Blavatsky, 1831-1891, Annie Besant 1847-1933, and Charles W. Leadbeater 1854-1934. They had written several books about the New Age Movement and psychic abilities, auras, and more. Annie Besant had written a book titled ***Esoteric Christianity*** and **Charles Leadbetter** and she had co-authored a book discussing the extensive colors of the human aura, called ***Thought Forms***. In 1875, Helena Blavatsky along with Henry Steel Olcott and William Quan Judge, founded the Theosophical Society which still exists today.

Besant was President of the Theosophy Society from 1907 until her death in 1933. Finally, I was learning so much more than the dogma that the traditional churches were teaching.

Over the years I have continued to read books on spiritual enlightenment and motivational improvement. One thing I learned was the church did not want any of their members to read religious literature that was not approved by the church. I have found this to be true of most of the major religions. But how can one learn the true meaning of life if you are not allowed to read all of the books on life. This brings a narrow-limited view of life. So, I read as much as I could. Now, I accept what I believe to be true and reject what I believe to be false. What I believe today is not necessarily what I believed yesterday and what I believe tomorrow may not be what I believe today. Madam Helena Blavatsky, said "There is no religion higher than *Truth.*" After 50 years of spiritual study I am ready to share with you what I have learned and What I Believe. In my writings I will offer nothing of my own, for everything I have learned comes from someone or something else. I cannot offer any plagiarism for everything I share has come from someone else and I will try to give credit where credit is due as often as I can. While we are on the subject of plagiarism, I need to explain how the human mind works and how to understand the concepts of this book. There are two parts to the human mind. First, we have the conscious mind which we use during our waking moments. The second part is the subconscious mind. The subconscious mind works 24 hours a day every minute every day. It never sleeps it is always active. When a newborn child first comes into this world, its conscious mind is completely empty. Just like a brand-new computer, before any software is loaded, its memory is completely blank. What makes a computer operate is a basic memory called ROM, that is; Read Only Memory. This ROM contains basic instructions for the computer to look for additional instructions on a hard disk, or a CD or DVD disk, or elsewhere. What makes a newborn's body work is the basic instructions in the subconscious mind. The basic instructions to make the body breathe, the heart to pump the blood, the digestive system to operate properly, other systems to expel the body's wastes, and any other instructions needed to keep the physical body and mental body completely operational. As we grow older and learn, we retain all this information, on life, in our conscious mind. Now, besides all the five physical senses that we use to input information into our mind, we impress our thoughts and actions on the subconscious mind. During the day if we have a particular problem we are trying to solve and it continues to repeat over and over in our conscious mind this thought, this idea, is impressed on the subconscious mind. If, at the end of the day the problem still exists and we go to sleep, the subconscious mind continues to work with the problem. Sometimes it finds an answer by searching memories within our own mind. Now comes the interesting part, and, this idea will be contested by many astute people. Often when the solution to a problem is not found by the subconscious mind, within the memory banks of the conscious mind, it looks for and sometimes receives the answer to the problem from the Universal Mind. This Creative Universal Mind is the understanding of the question- (is there intelligence in nature). We will discuss this subject of intelligence in nature as we continue in these writings.

So, you can see, with this field of thought, we

are all guilty of plagiarism. For we enter this world with nothing in our minds except our basic body functions. Everything we have learned comes from outside our physical mind except, any information we have gathered from the Universal Mind. In Helena Blavatsky's writings, she explained, that everything you have ever wanted to know is within, that is, it is within your own mind or the Universal Mind. You just have to learn how to look for the answer.

To continue our introduction for this writing, I need to mention the abilities of a certain author of some of the very interesting books I have read on the subjects of psychic experiences, the metaphysical, the intelligence of nature, spirit exchange, and aliens among us; **Ruth Montgomery** 1912-2001, was a writer of many books on spiritualism. She first started writing as a columnist covering politics and the U. S. White House during the Franklin Roosevelt administration. After several years in the press corps she had her first psychic experience while attending a séance that a friend insisted, she attend. Intrigued by her psychic experience she began to research psychic phenomenon and met Arthur Ford, a noted medium (psychic.) It was at this time that Ford told her that spirits had informed him that she was capable of receiving, psychically, information by way of automatic writing. This is a form of receiving information from the spirit world and recording it on paper called channeling. Usually the writer is not aware of the action of writing until it is finished. She started writing with pencil and paper until one day when the spirits took over the pencil and wrote; "WE SAID GO TO THE TYPEWRITER." Note; from - *The World to Come*, copyright 1999-page 12, published by Three Rivers Press, New York, N. Y. From then on, she wrote faster and more clearly. Since Montgomery's first encounter with the spirit world she has been recognized as a true spirit chaneller and published many books on the information she received. In this book she writes, several times, that the spirit guides have informed her that the twenty first century, that we have now started, is the beginning of a new era of enlightenment. Meaning, the world population is to begin to recognize mankind's proper place in the universe; that we are spiritual beings in a material universe. This, so called, age of enlightenment, according to some, is to usher in more self-realization, a time when much dogma of the major religions will cease to be taught and the self, will become less important than the whole of the population.

Continuing the introduction with the conscious, subconscious, and Universal Mind; I offer these writings on what I and many other writers and professional speakers believe. I believe there is one God, the one and only Creator of this universe. But, as you will see in these writings, I believe the one God does not punish and he does not reward. I believe we live under the laws of Mother Nature, Gravity and Karma, which is the Law of Attraction or the Law of Cause and Effect. Your life, your surroundings, your total environment in which you live, is the total result of everything in your past, everything you thought, said, and did. If you don't like your environment or the life you are leading, right now, you have the power to change it. By understanding and working with Karma, the Law of Attraction, you can change your life to anything you want. These writings of myself and many other writers will show you the way.

In creating that new environment in which we want to live, and changing ourselves, we need to understand the makeup of our intelligence and how it relates to Mother Nature's creative Universal Mind. As explained earlier, we have a conscious mind that we use during our waking moments, a subconscious mind we use 24 hours a day for our bodily functions, and, if we are successful, we can make that connection to the Creative Universal Mind. Now, throughout these writings you will read the word Secret. It is not a secret, at least not today. Maybe for years the Church tried to hide this information but today it is not a Secret, if you don't know it, you have just not been listening or have been reading the wrong books. Now we need to understand this, Secret, Natures Law of Attraction, or Cause and Effect, or Karma. By using the laws of Karma and repeating the same things over and over in the conscious mind, this thing we are concentrating on is impressed upon the subconscious mind and it will continue to work while we are sleeping, and, the subconscious mind will take those impressions or problems and impress them on the Creative Universal Mind looking for answers. Sometimes we receive our answers overnight, other times it takes longer. It is all part of how Karma and the Law of Attraction operate. You must continue this line of thinking knowing that you are a co-creator of your universe. Through the law of attraction, you can make it work. In your mind visualize the end result and create that feeling of success knowing, without a doubt, that success will be yours.

All the writers and books I will refer to have much of the same central theme I am trying to convey in this writing but, it is up to the reader to determine if it is appropriate for them. When you look for a new book study the index and introduction of the books, as I do, to learn if it may be acceptable for your journey of enlightenment. We each follow our own path. That is what the creator has given us, the power of choice. It is a great part of Karma, our guiding principle along with the laws and intelligence of Mother Nature. All this is a part of our journey of evolution. You, dear reader, are the Captain of your ship. You are the Chief Executive Officer of your enterprise. You make all the decisions in your life. No one else controls your life unless you let them. Now, begin to take control, study these writings that I and these authors offer you and build the life of your dreams. I seek **Truth** and try to express it- for this is **What I Believe-Truth.**

Notes

What I Believe-Truth
Chapter 1
Changing Times

As a new beginning, in the mid-19th century a new sense of religion was born. It was called New Age/New Thought, religious teachings, for what was being taught; metaphysics, reincarnation, and healing through the mind, was not necessarily accepted by the major religions at that time. Phineas P. Quimby, 1802- 1866, through discovering hypnotism, found that he could learn of ailments in other people's bodies possibly offering a cure. His writings were a great influence on the New Age movement. Edgar Cayce 1877- 1945 was an American Christian mystic and clairvoyant. Some people believe he was a strong leader in the new age movement. As a child he attended church often and read the Bible throughout. As a young man his psychic abilities grew stronger even to the point of professing to see auras around people, hearing voices of departed relatives, and speaking with angels. Edgar Casey became famous for his ability to put himself to sleep in a hypnotic state and then describe ailments and treatment for people with illnesses even though many of these patients were in a different locality than himself. It has been reported that twelve hundred of Edgar Cayce's psychic readings of patients and past and future events were documented.

Mary Baker Eddy, 1821- 1910, the founder of the Christian Science church, was also a part of the new age movement. Although today's church leaders will most likely deny this, in her early, years, she was a pupil of Phineas Quimby's, studied his writings, and was very interested in his ideas that the mind could create disease and could then cure the disease. This was totally not within the teachings of the major religions at the time. In 1875 Ms. Eddy wrote **Science and Health With Key to the Scriptures** which was her explanation of the Christian Bible. These writings are still used today daily by many believers. She established the First Church of Christ Scientists in Boston, Massachusetts, USA in 1879. The church today still teaches mind over matter can cure diseases.

In 1926 Ernest Holmes- 1887- 1960, published his book **Science of Mind**. In 1927 he founded the Church of Religious Science. Holmes was another New Age/New Thought thinker breaking from the old traditional church teachings and is reported to have studied the teachings of Quimby.

For more of what I believe and how it relates to New Age teachings, I offer the following from the book **Mind Power**, written by William Walker Atkinson. "I believe In the Supreme Principle Of Being the Infinite, Eternal Presence- Power for which all things proceed, and in which all things live and move and have their being. I believe in the Infinite Presence- Power even as I believe in my own existence; for I believe that my own existence is based and grounded in that Supreme Existence. Every report of my reason, and every report of my intuition, is to the effect that such Supreme Presence- Power exists, has always existed, and will always exist in Infinite Presence Power, an Identity-One unchangeable, Indivisible Reality. I do not base my belief upon dogmas nor upon the claimed authority of books or persons. I base it upon the inevitable, invariable, and infallible report of my own reason and intuition, from which all real belief must proceed. Reason is no foe to my faith it is rather one of its staunchest friends and allies."

William Walker Atkinson 1862- 1932.

It has been reported, in some circles, that the

New Age movement is evil. This could not be any further from the truth! The New Age/New Thought movement stresses One Supreme Being, the Creator of all there is and is the only- I Am That I Am. This is very much What I Believe and offer these writings on *What I Believe-Truth.*

Notes

What I Believe-Truth
Chapter 2
In The Beginning

A quick glance at Amazon's website reveals twelve authors who have written books on the subject of Lemuria, the lost continent. Lemuria or the land of Mu, supposedly a continent that existed in the middle of the Pacific- ocean between the American continent and Asia, flourished between 100,000 to 10,000 B.C. and then sank into the ocean. Fact or fiction I cannot say, the reader will have to judge for themselves. I offer the following as an interesting read; long before anything could have been written for the Bible, long before any religious prophet we have ever heard of even existed, long before any Sanskrit. From the book *The Lost Continent of Mu* (Lemuria) by Col. James Churchward- 1851- 1936, pages- 171- 191, "Originally, the universe was only a soul or spirit. Everything was without life- calm, silent, soundless. Void and dark, was the immensity of space. Only the Supreme Spirit, the great Self- Existing Power, moved within the abyss of darkness." "The desire came to Him to create worlds and

He created worlds; and the desire came to Him to create the earth, with living things upon it, and He created the earth and all therein." And this is the manner of the creation of the earth, with all the living things upon it. And he said; "let the gases which are without form and scattered through space be brought together, and out of them let the earth be formed." And the gases then assembled themselves into the form of a whirling mass. And he commanded; "Let the gases solidify to form the earth." Then the gases solidified; volumes were left on the outside, out of which water and the atmosphere were to be formed; and volumes were enveloped within the New World. Darkness prevailed and there was no sound, for as yet neither the atmosphere nor the waters were formed." And he commanded; "Let the outside gases be separated and let them form the atmosphere and the waters." And the gases were separated; one part went to form the waters, and the water settled upon the earth and covered its face so that no land anywhere appeared. The gases that did not form the waters formed the atmosphere, and the light was contained in the atmosphere. And the shafts of the sun met the shafts of the light in the atmosphere and gave birth to light. Then there was light upon the face of the earth; and the heat was also contained in the atmosphere. And the shafts of the sun met the shafts of the heat in the atmosphere and gave it life. Then there was heat to warm the face of the earth. And he commanded; "Let the gases that are within raise the land above the face of the waters." Then the fires of the under- earth lifted the land on which the waters rested until it appeared above the face of the waters, and this was the dry land. And he commanded; "Let life come forth in the waters." And the shafts of the sun met the shafts of the earth in the mud of the waters and there formed cosmic eggs (life germs) out of particles of the mud. Out of these cosmic eggs came forth life as commanded.

And he commanded; "Let life come forth upon the land." And the shafts of the sun met the shafts of the earth in the dust of the land, and out of it formed cosmic eggs; and from these cosmic eggs life came forth upon the earth as was commanded.

And when all this was done, he commanded; "Let us make man after our own image, and let us endow him with the powers to rule this earth." And then, the Creator of all things throughout the universe, created man, and placed within his body a living imperishable spirit, and man became like the creator in intellectual power. Then creation was complete."

For all of the above writings on the creation of our universe we are grateful to Col. James Churchward's book, *The Lost Continent of Mu*.

With over twenty years of study and travel he wrote the above words after discovering and deciphering ancient tablets written in an ancient language. A thousand tablets were discovered in a monastery in India. All the tablets had carved Naga symbols and characters which Churchward learned to decipher from a priest in India. Later, a Scottish geologist, William Niven, discovered over 2,000 stones with strange symbols he could not identify. After Niven contacted Churchward and described the symbols, Churchward confirmed they were the same as those on the tablets he and the priest had been deciphering. Besides the Naga writings found in India and South America, Churchward found the same symbols among the Hopi Indians in Colorado, USA.

These clay and stone tablets, that he read, may have been written more than 12,000 years ago in a land called Mu or Lemuria the lost continent now at the bottom of the Pacific

Ocean. Mu was a series of islands, a continent, that stretched from Peru South America to California to Hawaii and beyond almost to India and reportedly had a population of 64,000,000 people and prospered between 100,000 and 10,000 B.C. Legend says it submerged into the Pacific ocean during massive volcanic activity over 10,000 years ago. It is believed that the words of the Bible were taken from the more ancient writings after being taken from Mu to Burma, India, Greece, and Egypt. In 1926 Churchward published The Lost Continent of Mu. Much of Churchward's writings and his geological assumptions have been discredited by many authorities, stating they are absurd. Until proven otherwise I choose to believe there is some truth in this.

The writer Shirley Andrews- author of **Lemuria and Atlantis- Studying the Past to Survive the Future**, researched, for years, the stories of Lemuria and Atlantis. She communicated with many people who had claimed to have lived in these places in other lifetimes. Some claimed to have had vivid memories.

In deciphering these tablets Churchward determined that many of the inhabitants of Mu migrated both east and west and he reported that the "civilizations of India, Babylonia, Persia, Egypt, and Yucatan were but dying embers of the first great civilization." Also, in his book, *The Lost Continent of Mu*, p- 345, he wrote "there is the universality of certain old symbols and customs discovered in Egypt, Burma, India, Japan, China, South Sea Islands, Central America, South America and some of the North American Indian tribes and other seats of civilization. These symbols and customs are so identical it is certain they came from one source only--- Mu." Churchward also writes," p- 352- 378, "This continent, we find, was a vast stretch of rolling country, extending from North of Hawaii down towards the south, a line between Easter Island and the Fiji's formed its southern boundary. It was over 5000 miles from east to west, and over 3000 miles from north to south. The continent consisted of three areas of land, divided from each other buy narrow channels or seas."

Further he wrote, "there was a great continent in the middle of the Pacific Ocean where now we find only water and sky, and groups of small islands, which today are called the South Sea Islands. It was a beautiful, tropical country with vast plains. The valleys and the planes were covered with rich grazing grasses and tilted ferns, while the low rolling hill lands were shaded by luxuriant growths of tropical vegetation. No mountains or mountain ranges stretched themselves through this earthly paradise, for mountains had not yet been forced up from the bowels of the earth. The great rich land was intersected and watered by many broad, slow running streams and rivers, which wound their sinuous ways in fantastic curves and bends around the wooded hills and through the fertile plains. Luxuriant vegetation covered the whole land with a soft, pleasing, restful mantle of green. Bright and fragrant flowers on tree and shrub added coloring and finish to the landscape. Tall fronded Palm's fringed the oceans shores and lined the banks of the rivers for many a mile inland. Great feathery ferns spread their long arms out from the river banks. In Downey places where the land was low, the rivers broadened out into shallow lakes around whose shores, myriads of sacred lotus flowers dotted the listing service of the water. Like very colored jewels in settings of emerald green. Over the cool rivers, gaudy winged butterflies hovered in the shade of the trees, rising and falling in fairylike movements, as if better to view their painted beauty in nature's mirror. Darting hither and thither from flower to flower, hummingbirds made their short flights, glistening like living jewels in the rays of the sun. Feathered songsters and bush and tree vied with each other in their sweet lays. The chirping of lively crickets filled the air, while above all other sounds came those of the Locust as he industriously ground his scissors, telling the whole world, all was well with him. Roaming through the primeval forest were herds of mighty mastodons and elephants flapping their big ears to drive off annoying insects. The great continent was teeming with gay and happy life over which 64 million- human beings reigned supreme. All this life was rejoicing in its luxuriant home.

All followed the same religion, a worship of the deity through symbols. All believed the immortality of the soul, which eventually returned to the great source whence it came. So great was their reverence for the Deity they never spoke His name, and in prayer and supplication addressed Him always through a symbol. "Ra the sun" was used as the collective symbol for all His attributes.

As high priest Ra Mu was the representative of the Deity in religious teachings. It was thoroughly taught and understood that Ra Mu was not to be worshiped, as he was only a representative. At this time the people of Mu were highly civilized and enlightened. There was no severed tree on the face of the earth, nor had there ever been, since all the people on earth are children of Mu and under the certainty of the motherland."

Churchward continues in his narrative to describe the complexion of the race, the navigational skills of the sailors, there architectural and building skills and how they built great cities, towns, and villages scattered throughout the three lands. He continues to describe that through their navigational skills, trade, and commerce the land and the people flourished. He describes, in his book, that maybe over a period of 100,000 years, at different intervals, the land of Mu had experienced multiple volcanic eruptions. But after each time the surviving inhabitants rebuilt their cities. Later he describes the final terrible volcanic eruptions that destroyed the land of Mu which finally sank into the Pacific Ocean leaving only a few remaining scattered islands throughout the Pacific. One of those islands being the Easter Islands which contain the Easter Island monuments and one of the great puzzles of who built them and how were they built.

I offer all this previous information of a beautiful land of enlightened people that flourished between 100,000 and 10,000 years ago. In his writings Churchward wrote that throughout the ages learned priests, responsible for the history of mu, knew that the sacred information of mu needed to be protected. So, this information migrated east and west and was saved from destruction. All the religious teachings were never to be told to the common people. Only priests and the heir apparent to the throne were allowed to know these teachings. This practice continued in whatever land this information settled. Consequently, since Moses had been a prince in Egypt he would have been privy to all the ancient knowledge of mu and it is now surmised that Moses used this information 5,000 years- ago to write the book of Genesis. Churchward's description of the land of Mu sounds beautiful and delightful but Shirley Andrews book *Lemuria and Atlantis- Studying The Past To Determine The Future* and Ruth Montgomery's book *The World Before* tell us a slightly different story. They explain that humans on Lemuria were plagued by predatory animals including dinosaurs, therefore many people lived in caves or underground hovels which they burrowed out themselves. These provided some protection. They lived like this for thousands of years when they finally learned that since they could not kill the large adult dinosaurs they needed to search out and destroy their young. Eventually this gave them some relief.

All three writers confirmed in their writings that the inhabitants of Mu were very spiritual and worshipped one creator of the Universe. Churchward wrote they worshipped one Deity represented as Ra the Sun.

Edgar Cayce, Ruth Montgomery, and another spiritualist Tom T. Moore author of- *Atlantis and Lemuria- The Lost Continents Revealed*, received their information about the continents of Atlantis and Lemuria spiritually, and Shirley Andrews received her information from libraries and living people who claimed they had memories of past lives of these places. Ruth Montgomery explained that the Atlantean's had discovered and used extensive power from crystals, which included the power for ground and air vehicles and weapons of war. Multiple writers have written that the Atlantean's were very warlike and destroyed themselves while making experiments with powerful crystals. As for the destruction of the Lemuria, James

Churchward wrote that the Lemurians were a peaceful people and for thousands of years they had extensive earthquake and volcanic activity. And he reported the final act of destruction was the result of earthquakes and massive volcanic activity. It is believed that the destruction of Atlantis and Lemuria was somewhere between 30,000 and 10,000 BC. We don't know if all this destruction was at the same time. One more conjecture at this point is a writer explained that the massive devastation wrought by the sinking of the continents of Atlantis and Lemuria was the idea behind the world wide flood in the Holy Bible.

I have included the information in this chapter, **In The Beginning**, to show that much of the worldwide Spiritual information may have originated in the land of Mu, Lemuria. It appears that secret knowledge in the world community could have originated in Lemuria.

As an Update to this writing, I am including Information from the new book **Lifting The Veil On The Lost Continent Of Mu- The Motherland Of Men** copyright 2011 Reprinted 2013 by Jack Churchward the great-grandson Of Col. James Churchward. I offer the final summation on the rear cover of the book and I have included this writing in the Appendix A Recommended Authors and Writings. The rear cover reads as;

"A re-issue of the 1926 classic by James Churchward, The Lost Continent Of Mu: Motherland of Men supplemented with fresh research and new material by the author's great-grandson (Jack Churchward.) In the 1920's, James Churchward wrote a series of groundbreaking books about the continent of Lemuria which he called the land of Mu. The basic premises were The Garden of Eden was not in Asia, but on a sunken continent in the Pacific Ocean and the Biblical story of creation came not from the peoples of the Nile, but from this now submerged continent of Mu: The Motherland of Men.

He obtained the information by living with monks and translating unknown manuscripts. Over the years, his books have come to be considered occult classics. Now his great-grandson, Jack Churchward, has resurrected this valuable work and added his own research.

Subjects included are:

The Lost Continent-

The Land of Man's Advent on Earth

Egyptian Sacred Volume, Book of the Dead
Symbols of Mu
North American's Place Among the
Ancient Civilizations
The Geological History of Mu
Ancient Religious Conceptions
Ancient Secret Mysteries, Rights and
Ceremonies."

To continue now I offer the chapter **Nature's Intelligence –Intuition**; to show how understanding the intelligence of nature can lead us to a better understanding of Nature's Law of Attraction thereby allowing us to build a better life for ourselves.

Notes

What I Believe-Truth
Chapter 3
Nature's Intelligence- Intuition

There is no scientific explanation for intuition, what I call Nature's Intelligence. Intuition is that small voice within your mind. That feeling/idea that tells you something. Something is right or something is wrong. It is just knowing. We must learn to trust, or at least investigate, that feeling of intuition. In the case of animals, birds, fish, and insects, I suggest Intuition is the Intelligence of the Universal Mind. So, what is the explanation for the birth of a new kangaroo? How can we explain that, during birth, a kangaroo embryo, about the size of a lima bean, exits the birth canal, then proceeds upwards about 6 inches to find the mothers- pouch? This takes about three minutes while the infant travels through the mother's thick hair. Once inside the pouch the infant will search for and find a mother's teat, or nipple, for nourishment. The infant will remain attached to this nipple for upwards of 34 weeks. Every kangaroo offspring goes through the same procedure. So, we just explain this as intuition. This word, intuition, is a scientist's word for something they can't explain. In the case of an infant sea turtle's intuition, a female turtle lays her eggs ashore buried in the sand. Once the eggs hatch, the tiny ocean- going sea turtles head straight to the water. If a tiny female turtle should survive for as much as ten years they may return to the same nesting area where they were born to lay their eggs and continue the cycle of life. Again, scientists just call this intuition. But I would express a different explanation. There is a something within, a Universal Mind. In his book **Mind Power,** William Walker Atkinson writes about life and Mind Power being in everything. From the smallest tiny seed or even a grain of sand there is life in everything. If this is true then it confirms the idea that there is life in material objects that we would normally consider not alive such as rocks. In my experience with psychics and clairvoyance, I have been told, by some, they have spoken with the spirits in rocks, trees, and plants. In his book, **Mind Power**, Atkinson refers to the writings of Luther Burbank who examined plant life and said "all my investigations have led me away from the idea of a dead material universe tossed about by the various forces, to that of a universe which is absolutely all force life, soul or whatever name we choose to call it. Every atom, molecule, plant, or animal, is only an aggregation of organized unit forces held in place by stronger forces, thus holding them for a time latent, though teeming with inconceivable power. All life on our planet is, so, to speak, just on the outer fringe of this infinite ocean of force. The Universe is not half dead, but all alive."

Again, Atkinson writes "another writer Dr. Saleeby, in his book *Evolution: The Master Key,* goes even further in his claim of a living universe and life accompanied by mind. He says among other things "Life is potential in matter; life energy is not a thing unique and created at a particular time in the past. If evolution be true, living matter has been evolved by natural processes from matter, which is, apparently not alive. But if life is a potential in matter, it is 1000 times more evident that mind is potential in life, the evolutionist is impelled to believe that mind is potential in matter. The microscopic cell, a minute speck of matter that is to become man, has in it the promise and germ of mind. May we not then draw the inference that the elements of MIND are present in those chemical elements- carbon, oxygen, hydrogen, nitrogen, sulfur, phosphorus, sodium, potassium, and chlorine that are found in the cell. Not only must we do so, but we must go further, since we know that each of these elements, and every other, is built up out of one invariable unit, the electron, and we must therefore assert that mind is potential in the unit of matter, the electron itself."

To continue in this line of thinking that the electron itself contains information or the elements of mind, we can discuss briefly Bell's theorem. It seems that John Stuart Bell, the creator of Bell telephone and, I believe, the original patent holder and inventor of the electronic diode, created a theorem of quantum mechanics. Within this idea it was suggested that the electron contained memory and could transfer this memory to other electrons. At this point, of our treaties, I will leave this idea of electron intelligence for the readers further study of their' own.

We do not fully know or understand the mechanics of telepathy or spirit channeling. My own theory is that it is metaphysical, meaning, it is nonphysical and as a representative of mechanics an electron is physical. Though we cannot see an electron, still basically, we understand it to be physical or a representative of the material world.

Whatever the makeup of the spirit channelers or psychics or true clairvoyance it has been proven that much of the information they have presented is Truth. And, what we seek in these writings is Truth. Whatever operates telepathy, I believe it is spiritual not through the physical form of an electron.

Atkinson refers to the writings of a French scientist by the name of Nicholas Camille Flammarion who said; "The universe is a dynamism. Life itself, from the most rudimentary cell up to the most complicated organism, is a special kind of movement, a movement determined and organized by a directing force. Visible matter, which stands to us at the present moment for the universe, in which certain classic doctrines considered as the origin of all things, movement, life, thought is only a word void of meaning. The universe is a great organism, controlled by a dynamism of the physical order. Mind gleams through its every atom. There is mind in everything, not only in human and animal life but in plants, in minerals, in space." This is why we can say we live on a living planet.

A good starting point at understanding mind power is the worldwide bird, fish, and animal migration and hibernation when animals follow the sun for better feeding grounds. Billions of birds, fish, and animals do this every year traveling north, south, and wherever is necessary to find the best food sources for survival. We can call this a plan and a plan is- a sign of intelligence. If this intelligence is therefore world-wide, we can call it universal. A sign of intelligence usually suggests a mind; therefore, we can call this action a Universal Mind. Mother Nature directs every living thing on this planet. Nature directs all the animals, birds and fish in the migration for their survival.

Even plants have been found to have intelligence. **In Jeremy Narby's book** *Intelligence in Nature- An Inquiry Into Knowledge* **he writes**, "I had been looking into intelligence in nature for 18 months when a friend called me to draw my attention to a recent article in the Journal Nature. It claimed that the investigation of plant intelligence is" becoming a serious scientific endeavor: and that scientists are "only now beginning to express the remarkable complexity of plant behavior." These were the words of Anthony Trewavas, a professor of biology at the University Of Edinburgh and a fellow of the Royal Society, the oldest scientific society in Great Britain. According to Trewavas, plants have intentions, make decisions, and compute complex aspects of their environment.

I looked into the research cited by Trewavas and found, to my surprise, that scientists were now saying that plants have senses and can detect a wide variety of external variables, such as light, water, temperature, chemicals, vibrations, gravity, and sounds. They can also react to these factors by changing the way they grow. Plants can forage and compete with one another for resources. When attacked by herbivores, some plants signal for help, releasing chemicals that attract their assailant's predators. Plants can detect distress signals let off by other plant species and take preventative measures. They can assimilate information and respond on the whole-plant level. And they use cell-to-cell communication based on molecular and electrical signals, some of which are remarkably similar to those used by our own neurons. When a plant is damaged, it's cells send one another electrical signals just like our own pain messages."

Narby decided to interview Anthony Trewavas and **Trewavas' response to nature's intelligence begins with**, "Trewavas was already discussing the importance of plant intelligence, saying that scientists have long regarded plants as passive creatures, because they lack obvious movement. "Now to my mind, that assumption is wrong because it requires an equating of movement with intelligence. Movement is an expression of intelligence. It is not intelligence itself. Now, the definitions of intelligence are difficult..." "He spoke fluidly, needing no prompting to continue his line of thought. He said he found it necessary to peel away the human aspects that come with the notion of intelligence. In his view, our intelligence did not suddenly appear when we became Homo sapiens. It evolved from other organisms. Hence the importance of defining intelligence in a way that does not apply exclusively to humans. Trewavas referred to the definition devised in 1974 by New Zealand philosopher and psychologist David Stenhouse, who described intelligence as "adaptively- variable behavior within the lifetime of the individual." This can apply to many different organisms and means non-instinctive behavior that maximizes the individual's fitness." **Narby said, during the interview,** "he (Trewavas) said he had spent years pondering the behavior of plants in the light of Stenhouse's definition. Though most plants do not move at a speed perceptible to the naked eye, they respond as individuals to signals from their environment and develop an adaptively- variable way. Even plants growing in pots inside houses turn their leaves to the light to optimize light collection and send the roots down in the soil and their shoots up into the air. And wild plants manage to compete with other plants for resources. Research now shows that growing shoots can sense neighboring plants. They can detect shifts in infrared light indicative of nearby greenery, predict the consequences of that presence, and take evasive action. Plants can alter the shape and direction of their stems to maintain an optimal position relative to sunlight. They can adjust their growth and development to maximize their fitness in a variable environment. According to Trewavas, this means they are intelligent, if one refers to Stenhouse's definition."

Narby continued, "I asked Trewavas if he thought plants think when they make decisions. He replied that he did not. In his opinion, they compute what is actually going on, then make appropriate responses in terms of what they perceive.

Having answered my question, he continued making the case for plant plasticity. Plants have to gather resources in their local environment while facing competition from their neighbors. As they are mainly fixed in one place, the most sensible way any plant can do this is to occupy the space around itself in an optimal way. A branching structure happens to be the simplest way in which this can be done, and this is the solution plants adopt both below ground, as they send down roots into the soil to form exploitative tissues and above ground, as they deploy their leaves to gather the maximum amount of light. To do all this, an individual plant must perceive a gravity vector and align itself correctly, and it's actual shape and morphology are determined by the quantity and quality of light it perceives. For Trewavas, this is "adaptively variable behavior within the lifetime of the individual, i.e., Intelligence. "Furthermore, individual plants do not choose their environment, as seeds land and germinate where they can. Plants have to grow in a great variety of environments and adjust their structures to optimize their ability to exploit what they find."

In another section of Jeremy Narby's book, ***Intelligence in Nature- An Inquiry Into Knowledge,* he writes** of his trip in the forests and rivers of the Peruvian Amazon which contains an abundance of "more species of trees, insects, reptiles, amphibians, birds, and mammals than any other region of similar size." Narby and several other scientists and anthropologists were investigating local parrot activities in a particular region of this Peruvian forest. He and the other investigators were staying at the Lodge called the Matsigenka Center for Tropical Studies. During his initial stay he met a gentleman named Charlie Munn. Who presented himself and said he had done his doctoral research in the nearby Manu Biosphere Reserve. He had worked with the Matsigenka Indians "and his team discovered that macaws, the colorful giants of the parrot world, gathered daily for most of the year at large banks of clay, which they peck at and consume in small morsels." **Narby's writing continues** "he (Munn) said he and his research team were initially mystified by the Macaws consumption of clay. They assumed the clay contained salts and minerals that supplement the birds primarily vegetarian diet. Then a graduate student analyzed the seeds commonly eaten by the macaws and discovered they contain toxic alkaloids. Macaws preferred eating the seeds of fruit to their pulp, and they use their powerful, hooked beaks to crack and consume seeds from many different trees, unlike most birds in the tropical forest. It turns out, Munn said, that the clay the birds eat, binds to these toxins and speeds their elimination from the body, and probably also lines the gut and protects it from the chemical erosion by the seeds' toxins. Macaws take almost daily doses of clay to detoxify themselves, which allows them to eat foods that other animals cannot tolerate. He added that macaws choose clays with a much higher capacity to bind toxins than adjacent bands of clay, which they shun. They prefer clays rich in kaolin, which humans use to cure food poisoning."

Later, Charlie Munn, invited Narby on the next outing to observe the actions of the macaw parrots. Narby then explains the actions of the observations, "by the time we reached the clay lick, daylight was almost breaking. Toyeri (their guide) took us to the base of a 50- yard cliff made of reddish clay and ushered us into a sizable blind made of palm leaves. The bird watchers were all there and had deployed their cameras and powerful binoculars on tripods. The blind had the feel of a nest of spies. We were told to be quiet, because the macaws and other parrots were due to appear any time, and visible or audible human presence would keep them away." Not caring for the condition of this blind he and his guide proceeded to another location, where he writes, "We hid under tree cover in a spot that allowed us to peek out through the vegetation and catch a panoramic view. The clay cliff in front of us began to echo with bird calls, chirps, and squawks. It sounded like an aviary. Out of nowhere, hundreds of birds had congregated. I closed my eyes and listened. The sound reminded me of the scene in Hitchcock's film The Birds, in which thousands of seagulls flocked together and let off a threatening din. But these macaws sounded raucous and celebratory, rather than threatening.

During a pause in the sound recording, I asked Toyeri (the guide) to name some of the birds we were hearing. He pulled out the "Birds of Columbia" book from his shoulder bag and started reeling off names in English, which I noted down: scarlet macaws, blue and gold macaws, chestnut fronted macaws, white eyed parakeets, yellow and crowned parrots, blue headed parrots... The cliff had become a wall of spinning rainbow colors. The racket the birds made was both symphonic and deafening. As they hung out on the red clay cliff, they also appeared to squabble, tumble off, and dive-bomb one another, twirling. and pirouetting, while other birds flew over to nearby trees letting out loud screeches. Magnificent colors and movements blended with dissonant sounds and a dazzling spectacle. I asked Toyeri what he thought the birds were saying to one another. He replied, in Spanish, "they are all friends. They make such noise when they eat clay because they are saying- "everybody come over here, it's really good here," for them, the minerals and salts are all like sweets for us. It is their food. They do this from 5:30 to 715, then they all go their separate ways to the forest. This is like their breakfast." Narby continues, "The parrots get together came to an end as abruptly as it began. The birds started flying off in different directions over the forest. Within minutes, the party was over, and a crowd of about 1000 had dwindled to a handful of individuals. My watch indicated 7:15, these birds were punctual."

Jeremy Narby's investigations of the Macaw parrots continues to show the intelligence in nature, how else do we explain the actions of the parrots in which they consumed the clay to expel the toxins that they eat throughout the day. Another example of intelligence in nature is leaf-cutter ants. **Narby writes the following;** "even creatures with tiny brains have astonishing capacities. For example, leaf cutter ants, with brains the size of a grain of sugar, practice underground agriculture and use antibiotics wisely – and appear to have been doing so for 50 million years. Living in the South and Central American rain forests, these ants feed themselves by getting around plant defenses with the help of a mushroom. They cut vegetation, scrape away plant antifungal defenses such as the waxy coating of leaves, chew the leafy matter into a pulp, and use it as a substrate on which they grow their antifungal crops. In turn, the fungus does away with the insecticide substances contained in the leaves, which it digests, and which are absent from the mushroom tissue eaten by the ants. A leaf cutter nest is mainly underground, an excavated Warren with thousands of chambers filled with gray fungus. Warrens can reach the size of a human living room and house up to 8 million ants. The fungus is the ant's main food, and they make a monoculture of it. This puts their underground farms at the mercy of parasites and pests. One parasite in particular is a devastating species of mold that is found only in antifungal gardens. Leaf cutter ants do not just weed, manure, and prune their fungal crops; they also work constantly to keep the parasite mold in check. To do this, scientist recently discovered, they use Streptomyces bacteria, which they carry on specialized parts of their bodies. This particular bacterium is a source of half the antibiotics used in medicine. Ants appear to have been using antibiotics on their fungal crops for millions of years without developing the pathogen resistance that plagues human use of antibiotics. How could they do this without a form of intelligence? Defining "intelligence" is problematic, and I spent several days looking into the question. I found that intelligence has often been defined in terms of human capacities. Definitions include: "the ability to solve problems or to create products that are valued within one or more cultural settings, "or" a bio psychological potential of our species to process certain kinds of information in certain kinds of ways, "or" skill in the use of a medium (like computers or symbol systems)"

Author's note; (A symbol system can be used in the development of AI- artificial intelligence.) "These definitions imply that other species lack intelligence. Other definitions emphasize the multiplicity of intelligences – linguistic, logical – mathematical, emotional, musical, practical, spatial, and so on. Intelligence has also been defined as the capacity for abstraction. Anthropologists have pointed out that some cultures have no concept for intelligence, while others define it in ways surprising to Westerners, for example, in terms of good listening skills, or a strong sense of ethics, or the ability to observe, interpret, and negotiate the social and physical landscape. Intelligence is an elusive concept. In such cases I usually turn to the etymology of words. In its original meaning, intelligence refers to choosing between- (inter-legere)- and implies the capacity to make decisions."

We are Greatly indebted to Jeremy Narby for writing this great book on the intelligence of nature. These actions of animals, birds, fish, plants, and ants should help us understand our relationship to nature. It has been said that, overall, the human earthly population has forgotten its relationship to nature. It seems, that this started when we became urbanized and many of us started living in towns and cities and especially when we created artificial illumination. When streetlights were invented it started the disappearance of stars. As villages became towns, towns became cities, cities became metropolises, we were unable to see the stars above us. Many humans who live in large cities today never see the stars in the sky or hardly ever see trees and plants and very few animals.

There was a news story some time ago that in the city of Los Angeles, while they had experienced an electric grid power failure and all electricity was out of service, hundreds of telephone calls were received by the 911 emergency system. It seems that the general public was reporting a bright light in the sky and people could not identify this bright light. The public was then informed, by local scientists, that the bright light in the sky was the star constellation the Milky Way. We have forgotten our connection to nature. We must remember to appreciate nature, that nature has a plan for everything on this planet and wants abundance in everything and yet at the same time requires balance in all. Even for us, while our bodies and minds enjoy abundance, we must also have balance. If we have too much food, we become overweight. If we don't have enough exercise, we become lethargic and our bodies can even experience ill health. We even must exercise our minds keeping ourselves active and attentive to all of our environment.

Now that we have seen examples of the intelligence of nature it should help explain this intelligence of the Universal Mind. This intelligence leads us now to our next chapter on Conversing With The Universal Mind.

Notes

What I Believe-Truth
Chapter 4
Conversing With The Universal Mind

When we meditate, we need to close the physical surroundings from our mind. We don't need to listen to the hustle and bustle of the world around us. We just need to be quiet and listen for an inner voice. In my past experience, when I have tried to receive guidance from a superior consciousness, I have, many times, been very disappointed that, I thought, I never received an answer from God or my guardian angel. In other words I felt my prayers were not answered. How extremely disappointing it is when you feel your prayers are not answered. But it seems I was listening the wrong way. From what I have read and what I have learned through this communing with our spirit guides or guardian angels, we must learn how to listen. It is difficult to listen when you don't know how. For example, next time you have a chance to sit quietly and read something, pronounce the words in your own mind. Listen to that inner voice. So, when you ask a question in your mind during your prayers listen for that inner voice. Although the inner voice is there in your mind it may come through more as just an idea and not a physical sound. You won't hear the physical sound with your ears. It is more like an idea coming to you in your mind. Very often when you're working on a project in your mind and concentrating on the physical things to do or maybe even concentrating on the words you need to use for your writings you may suddenly receive a new idea. That, most likely, is your inner voice, your intuition, coming to you from the Universal Mind. We must learn to recognize and appreciate this information that comes to us from the Universal Mind. This Universal Mind/idea can be demonstrated by the ideas on how human flight, the airplane, and the automobile were brought to fruition on this earth. As one person began working on the idea of building an airplane the idea was presented to the Universal Mind and many of those ideas became accessible to other persons as they started thinking about flight. This same idea, of a connection to the Universal Mind, came about when Henry Ford built his first assembly

line and created automobiles thusly.
Eventually the idea of automobiles and the assembly lines became universal. All because the information was available to all of mankind.

We can make this connection to the Universal Mind by concentrating on whatever it is that we desire. I would not suggest meditating while driving or operating machinery or even playing sports when our concentration is needed elsewhere. But if we are in a situation where we can concentrate, we can, quietly, think about what it is we want, concentrating on that idea, and then quietly listen for an answer. An answer may come to us suddenly as a new idea, not necessarily in words but just a thought. But then again, we may not receive an answer at all. We may ask for the information we need but if we receive no answer just let it go. Quietly continue on and expect that you will receive an answer later on when you least expect it. Very often this happens to me when I will request an answer for a particular problem but receive no answer at that particular time than later throughout my day when doing something totally different I may suddenly receive an answer for my previous question. But in this situation, we must learn to recognize the answer was provided.

When communing with Spirit and the Universal Mind we must learn to appreciate and give thanks for any guidance we receive. Thankfulness and gratitude are two very important things in your life. When you give thanks to the spirit world for all the good in your life you will receive more goodness in your life. And just the opposite is true, if you are unhappy in your life and have despair you may receive more unhappiness and more despair through the laws of Karma. Always maintain that positive attitude knowing that your spirit guides and your guardian angels are watching over you and are available to you to help guide you on your journey of evolution.

Notes

What I Believe-Truth
Chapter 5
The Law of Attraction

This Creative Universal Mind is the Intelligence we connect to when we confront the Law of Attraction in creating a better life for ourselves.

Once again, I remind you- you are the cocreator of your universe/your world. Now use this power of positive thinking to create the world in which you want to live.

Napoleon Hill, 1883- 1970, wrote two books. His first was called *The Law of Success* and his second was called *Think and Grow Rich*. The second book sold over 20 million copies. For more than 20 years Napoleon Hill interviewed very successful people including presidents Woodrow Wilson, Theodore Roosevelt, and Franklin Delano Roosevelt trying to find the secret of success. Many of the successful men he interviewed said there was a something within, but could not explain it further. This secret- the something within called mind- power, is God's gift to us that allows us to build beautiful mansions or skyscrapers, or spaceships that fly to the moon.

We live breath, move, and have our being within the grace of God, the One Creator. God does not punish nor does he reward us for what we do. I believe that when God created man God gave man the power of choice. We have the choice of how we live our lives and we live under the law of nature, what the Hindus call Karma, Cause and Effect. We call this nature's Law of Attraction.

Cause and Effect or nature's Law of Attraction is in the Bible; Matthew 7, 7- "Ask, and it shall be given you; seek, and ye shall find; knock, and it shall be opened unto you: 7, 8- "For every one that asketh receiveth; and he that seeketh findeth; and to him that knocketh it shall be opened."

Mark 11, 24- "Therefore I say unto you, what things so ever ye desire, when ye pray, believe that ye receive them, and ye shall have them."

Proverbs; 23, 7 "For as he thinketh in his heart so is he."

This is what Earl Nightengale called "the greatest secret ever told; you are what you think about."

This idea that "you are what you think" is over

2,000 years old. Even before Master Jesus taught this Buddha said "The Mind Is Everything, what you think, you become." Gautama Buddha lived from 483 to 400 BC. Many of the books I recommend for understanding the Law of Attraction were written over 100 years ago.

When we ask for something, we use the Law of Attraction, we must believe that it will happen. Having faith and knowing that nature will provide is the key to receiving what we ask for.

So how do we create success in our life? Napoleon Hill, followed the practices of the new thought tradition. In his first book published in 1928 the **Law Of Success**, his first venture into motivational enlightenment through mind- power, he introduced a set of 15 principles that he learned from successful industrialists, diplomats, and other successful people. Most of these 15 principles seem to be guiding you toward being the best possible employee of some large corporation. He stresses one important principle as imagination. Use your imagination to obtain a successful result. Then he stresses a definite chief aim, self-confidence the habit of saving, initiative and leadership, enthusiasm, self-control, a habit of doing more than paid for, a pleasing personality, accurate thought concentration, cooperation, how to accept failure, tolerance, and a golden rule.

The original version was an eight- volume set. My copy contains 598 pages. This volume was initially successful but, his most successful writing was the book "Think and Grow Rich." It was first published in 1937 and sold over 20 million copies. Hill gained his knowledge for writing these two books by interviewing very successful people.

Which were the likes of President Woodrow Wilson, President Franklin Delano Roosevelt, Andrew Carnegie, Henry Ford, Alexander Graham Bell, Thomas Edison, John D Rockefeller, Harvey Samuel Firestone, Theodore Roosevelt, Charles M Schwab, F. W. Woolworth, William Wrigley Jr., and many others. He studied all these people to learn the secret of their success and what was that something within, that allowed them to obtain such heights of success.

Hill presented his findings in chapters consisting of things like Desire, Faith, Knowledge, Imagination, Planning, Persistence, and Intuition (The Sixth Sense.) In other words, a well-defined plan of business.

Another well-known writer, **Deepak Chopra**

wrote a book called **The Seven Spiritual Laws of Success**. His chapters consisted of potential, giving, karma, effort, intention, purpose and how to succeed.

After many years of studying Cause and Effect, nature's Law of Attraction, I have arrived at my own set of principles for achieving any set goal. They are;

1. Idea- at first comes the idea of a project or a desired result of something you want. You then select that idea for your desired result.

2. Desire- you now must learn of your true desire for this project, or final results of what you are seeking.

3. Decide- now you must decide if this is what you truly want. You must be absolutely sure in your decision.

4. Plan- now that the decision has been made of what you desire you must make the plans to achieve the end results.

5. Goals- you have an idea, desire, and the decision to achieve this desire. Now you must plan and work toward all the goals needed for achievement.

6. Faith- having faith is mandatory. Don't just think you can do this but Know through absolute certainty of your success. Have faith in yourself, know that you can accomplish your goals.

7. Believe- along with Faith, you must absolutely believe, without any doubt, that you will achieve your goals.

8. Work- now comes the physical or mental work needed to achieve the end results.

9. Discipline- tying in all the previous principles including the actual work requires complete discipline. Work as often as you can toward your goals.

10. Persistence- discipline, work, believing, faith, goals, planning, decisions, desire, and that indestructible idea, leads us to;

11. Achievement- having attained our results will lead us to;

12. Abundance- success.

Along with these instructions one must use **VISUALIZATION and Affirmation.** Make a mental picture of your idea and each goal. Then **Visualize and Affirm,** that is, **Know** that you will achieve the desired results of your goal. By having faith in yourself and **KNOWING** that you can accomplish your dreams you bring in the power of the **Universal Mind** to help you accomplish your goals.

An example of the practical theory of The Law of Attraction is the spiritual counselor and writer Florence Scoville Shinn. Her book *The Game of Life- and How to Play It* is a series of counseling's she gave to individuals. Each person she counseled had a particular problem of which they were unable to solve. Through teaching them the power of the Law of Attraction they were able to overcome their problems and achieve success. Every person that teaches the law of attraction shows us that the law has no favorites. Good or bad, positive or negative, whatever you think or say can come true. A simple little story Shinn tells us in her book is a gentleman complained that every time he went to ride the trolley, he was always late and missed the first one. Then he had to wait to catch the next trolley. But his daughter told Shinn that every time she arrived at the trolley station she was always on time and never missed her trolley. That is the power of positive and negative thinking. Dr. Norman Vincent Peale, an American minister, titled his book on the Law of Attraction, *The Power of Positive Thinking.* In Shinn's book, this young girl expressed the positive attitude knowing she would always make her trolley and, her father expressed the negative attitude when he expected to miss his trolley every time. We must constantly monitor our thoughts to keep them positive and be sure we don't express negativity.

In another situation a lady came to Shinn and

said she wanted to move to New York City but all her friends told her there were no available apartments in New York everything was taken, she might as well stay where she is. But she insisted she wanted to move to New York City. Shinn informed her to continue to think positive and plan accordingly, knowing that she would find the right apartment. So, she went to a local store selected furniture and the necessary household items for her new apartment and went home and kept the strong positive thoughts knowing that she would receive the right apartment. Soon she received a message informing her that an apartment had unexpectedly become available and it was offered to her. Now that was the power of positive thinking. Selecting the furniture and things she needed for a new apartment and keeping those positive thoughts knowing that the law of attraction would provide what was necessary. MS. Shinn's book tells us many stories like this. All the writers and motivational speakers that teach the Law of Attraction tell us the same basic theme; our creator, the one God, has created this world for us with Nature's laws. We have a Law of Gravity, a law of Gratitude, a Law of Attraction (Karma) and we have been given the power of choice. All perfect laws to live by. Just like the Law of Gravity, the Law of Attraction does not have punishment. If you step into a hole you will fall down. Miss a step on a set of steps you will fall down. If you put your hand in a fire you will be burned. This is not punishment. It is only a reaction. It is the same with the Law of Attraction. Everything you think reacts to you. When you have good, happy thoughts, good returns to you. You may not experience physical results but nonetheless you may have a pleasant experience. Wake up angrily when that alarm clock goes off in the morning and you throw it across the room, you may stub your tow as you get out of bed or you may spill your coffee on your best clothes as you rush out the door on the way to work. Don't think angry thoughts, keep those positive thoughts always active in your mind. The two most personal dangers in any individual's life are anger and depression. They invite all types of negativity into our lives. We must constantly control our minds to remain positively centered.

There is a story about an old man. A senior citizen who was living in a very nice senior living or assisted living quarters where he was very happy in his senior years. Then, things changed, due to certain circumstances, he was moved to another facility that was not as nice. But he was always happy. When asked how he always remained happy when he had been moved to a place that was not as nice as before, he replied, "Every morning, when I wake and put my feet on the floor, I have a choice to be happy or to be sad. I choose to be happy." This is a good rule to live by. Every day, every minute, and every second we are given a choice of what we can think. Our thoughts create our life, our tomorrows. Constantly monitor your thoughts to keep them positive. Choose to be happy instead of sad and create the good life.

In 2006, Rhonda Byrne published her book *The Secret* and she created a video with the same title. She, along with Twenty-four professional speakers, presented a great work on the Law of Attraction. I highly recommend you buy the video and the book. I have both and refer to them often. It is a good start on your journey to a better life.

All writers and speakers of the Law of Attraction tell us; whatever you are experiencing in life today, whatever surrounds you, is the result of all your thoughts in the past and, to change your circumstances you need, only, to change your thoughts. You can have; good health, be anything you want, live

wherever you want, have miraculous healing, abundance, fame, friends, family, companionship and anything you can vision. But the Law of Attraction works both ways. You must guard your mind against negative thoughts because these can come true also. In Rhonda Byrne's book *The Secret* you will find quotations from the following professional speakers; John Assaraf, Michael Bernard Beckwith, Lee Brower, Jack Canfield, Robert Collier, Dr. John F. Demartini D.C., B.S.C., Marie
Diamond, Mike Dooley, Bob Doyle, Hale Dwoskin,
Morris Goodman, John Gray, PhD., Charles Haanel, John Hagelin, PhD., Bill Harris, Dr. Ben
Johnson MD, N.M.D., Loral Langemeir, Prentice
Mulford, Lisa Nichols, Bob Proctor, James Arthur
Ray, David Schimer, Marci Shimoff, MBA, Dr. Joe
Vitale MSC.D., Dr. Dennis Whaitley PhD, Neale
Donald Walsh, Wallace Wattles, Fred Alan Wolf PhD.,
At the end of this book, in Appendix A, you will

find a list of these speakers/writers and links to their books.

This Law of Attraction that I speak of is referred to slightly differently in Dr. Wayne W. Dyer's book ***The Power Of Intention- Learning To Co-create Your World Your Way*** in this he explains this power of intention and maintaining positive thoughts of abundance. He writes; "Abundance is the natural state of the nature of intention. Your desire for abundance must flow free of resistance. Any discrepancy between your individual intention or desire, and your belief concerning the possibility of summoning it into your life, creates resistance. If you want it but believe it's impossible or that you are unworthy, or that you don't have the skills or perseverance, then you created resistance and you're disallowing. Your feelings indicate how well you're attracting the energy necessary for the fulfillment of your desire strong feelings of despair, anxiety, blame, hate, fear, shame, and anger are sending you the message that you want success and abundance but you don't believe it's possible for you. These negative feelings are your clues to get busy and balance your desires with those of the universal mind of intention, which is the only source of that which you desire. Negative emotions tell you that you're pulling power from intention is weak or even nonexistent. Positive emotions tell you that you're connecting to and accessing the power of intention.

Concerning abundance, one of the most effective ways to increase that pulling power from intention to you is to take the focus off of dollars and place it on creating abundant friendship, security, happiness, health, and high energy. It's here that you'll begin to feel those higher emotions, which let you know that you're back in the match game with the all-creating Source. As you focus on having abundant happiness, health, security, and friendship, the means for acquiring all of this will be flowing toward you. Money is only one of those means, and the faster your vibrational energy around abundance radiates, the more money will show up in significant amounts. These positive feelings, as indicators of your pulling power for success and abundance, will put you into an active mode for co-creating your intentions."

A part of the Law of Attraction is gratitude. If you want more of what is good in your life be grateful. If you don't want to be grateful to God then be grateful to Mother Nature. You must choose to live in a place of gratitude, greater peace, and higher consciousness, you must learn to follow your desires, do what you love and take time to give gratitude for all you have and more of everything will come to you. It is your natural birthright to be happy.

In support of abundance I offer the follow;

Wallace D. Wattles in his book, *The Science of Getting Rich*, **writes,** at the very beginning of his book, "Whatever may be said in praise of poverty, the fact remains that it is not possible to live a really complete or successful life unless one is rich. No one can rise to his greatest possible height in talent or soul development unless he has plenty of money, for to unfold the sole and to develop talent he must have many things to use, and he cannot have these things unless he has the money to buy them with.

A person develops in his mind, soul, and body by making use of things, and society is so organized that man must have money in order to become the possessor of things. Therefore, the basis of all advancement must be the science of getting rich.

The object of all life's development, and everything that lives has an inalienable right to all the development it is capable of attaining. A person's right to life means his right to have the free and unrestricted use of all the things which may be necessary to his fullest mental, spiritual, and physical unfoldment; or, in other words, his right to be rich.

In this book, I shall not speak of riches in a figurative way. To be really rich does not mean to be satisfied or contented with the middle. No one ought to be satisfied with a little if he is capable of using and enjoying more.

The purpose of nature is the advancement and unfoldment of life, and everyone should have all that can contribute to the power, elegance, beauty, and richness of life. To be content with less is sinful.

The person who owns all he wants for the living of all the life he is capable of living is rich, and no person who has not plenty of money can have all he wants. Life has advanced so far and become so complex that even the most ordinary man or woman requires a great amount of wealth in order to live in a manner that even approaches completeness.

Every person naturally wants to become all that they are capable of becoming. This desire to realize innate possibilities is inherent in human nature; we cannot help wanting to be all that we can be. Success in life is becoming what you want to be. You can become what you want to be only by making use of things, and you can have the free use of things only as you become rich enough to buy them. To understand the science of getting rich is therefore the most essential of all knowledge. There is nothing wrong in wanting to get rich. The desire for riches is really the desire for a richer, fuller, and more abundant life, and that desire is praiseworthy.

The person who does not desire to live more abundantly is abnormal, and so the person who does not desire to have money enough to buy all he wants is abnormal.

There are three motives in which we live: we live for the body, we live for the mind, we live for the sole. No one of these is better or holier than the other; all are alike desirable, and no one of the three- body, mind, or soul- can live fully if either of the others is cut short or of full life and expression. It is not right or noble to live only for the sole and deny mind or body, and it is wrong to live for the intellect and deny body or soul."

"It is in the use of material things that a person finds full life for his body, develops his mind, and unfolds his soul. It is therefore of supreme importance to each individual to be rich."

In wanting to obtain abundance and riches we must learn how to use this Law of Abundance.

You must tell the Universal Mind that you want something but, never say or think that you do not want a something. You never say- Spirit, I'm going on a picnic today and I don't want any rain.

Instead, you should say Spirit, I'm going on a picnic today and I know it will be a beautiful day. If you have been searching for a new home and you find one that seems to be just the right one for you but in the back of your mind you say to yourself, I love this house but I cannot afford it. That is the wrong thing to say. Spirit hears you say- I cannot afford it. That is a negative statement. We want a positive statement. What you need to say is Spirit, I know that Spirit will provide me with the right house at the right time and in the right way.

When you want more good things in your life, many motivational speakers and writers have said, and written, you need to create a wishing board. This is when you take a poster board and find magazine pictures of things you want and places where you want to go. For instance, if you want a new car find a picture of just the right car you want. The correct style, the correct brand, and the right color just for you. Cut that out and paste it on the poster

board. Think of just the right vacation spot for you, find a picture of it and paste
it on the poster board. If you want more money, find a picture of piles of money cut it out and paste it on your board. Think of all the things you want and places you want to go to. Find the appropriate pictures and paste them on your poster board then, throughout the day, look at that board frequently and know, that all these things will come true, and Spirit will provide all these things at the right time and in the right way.

I highly recommend that you read **Jack Canfield**'s book- ***Key to Living the Law of Attraction-A Simple Guide to Creating the Life of Your Dreams***. In this he writes all the how to's in creating the life of your dreams. Affirmations, gratitude, visualization, purpose, all that keeps you focused on your desires. Through meditation, contemplation and visualization, anytime day or night, you become more attuned to Spirit and more ideas about what you want and what you want to do will come to you. You must learn to recognize these new ideas as they just seem to pop into your mind. The more you think about your subject and the more you do, the more ideas you will receive.

Along with recommending **Jack Canfield**'s

book **Key to Living the Law of Attraction**, I must also recommend his book ***The Success Principles – How to Get from Where You Are to Where You Want to Be*** and the audio version also.

This Universal Mind, the intelligence of Nature, is the force that drives our world. This force is what Napoleon Hill called that Something Within. William Walker Atkinson called this something within the Divine Presence– Power. In his book ***The Complete Wallace D. Wattles*** and in his book ***The Science OF Getting Rich*** he writes about this Something Within when he wrote; "There is a thinking stuff from which all things are made, and which, in its original state, permeates, penetrates, and fills the inter spaces of the universe. A thought in this substance produces the thing that is imaged by the thought.

A person can form things in his thought, and, by impressing his thought upon formless substance, can cause the thing he thinks about to be created. In order to do this, a person must pass from the competitive to the creative mind; he must form a clear mental picture of the things he wants, and hold this picture in his thoughts with the fixed PURPOSE to get what he wants, and the unwavering FAITH that he does get what he wants, closing his mind against all that may tend to shake his purpose, dim his vision, or quench his faith."

Other books with the **Complete Wallace D. Wattles** are; The Science OF Being Great, The Science OF Being Well, How To Get What You Want, A New Christ, Jesus: The Man And His Work, Making The Man Who Can (How To Promote Yourself), The New Science Of Living And Healing.

Dr. Wayne W. Dyer, 1940- 2015, wrote a New York Times best-selling book titled **The Power of Intention– Learning to Co-create Your World Your Way** in which he called the Something Within, the all creating Source and named it The Power of Intention. In naming eight chapters in the Contents page he calls these chapters; It Is My Intention to:

- Respect Myself at All Times
- Live My Life on Purpose
- Be Authentic and Peaceful with All of My Relatives
- Feel Successful and Attract Abundance into My Life
- Live a Stress-Free Tranquil Life
- Attract Ideal People and Divine relationships
- Optimize My Capacity to Heal and Be Healed

- Appreciate and Express the Genius That I AM

Dyers words throughout his book are very similar to the meanings of what the other writers have used as we have explored the Law of Attraction and how to bring the good things in life you want into your life. He has only substituted Intention for Attraction. In one section he writes "I feel successful, I intend to feel the abundance that is here, now." "I am success; I am abundance. When you're success itself, when you're abundance itself, you're in harmony with the all-creating Source, and it will do the only thing it knows how to do. It will be endlessly giving and forthcoming with that which has no resistance to it – namely, you."

Now I would like to introduce you to the book titled; *Success Secrets of the Motivational Superstars* by Michael Jeffreys copyright 1996. Jeffreys interviewed and then wrote about 15 of the most successful motivational speakers of the United States at that time. They are; Anthony Robbins, Dr. Wayne W Dyer, Barbara De Angelis, Ph.D., Brian Tracy, Les Brown, Mark Victor Hansen, Roger Dawson, Tom Hopkins, Jack Canfield, Joel Weldon, Danielle Kennedy, Mike Ferry, Art Linkletter, Patricia Fripp, and Leo Buscaglia.

In Jeffreys introduction he writes; "this is a book about 15 individuals who dared to dream big, and then had the audacity to go out and turn that dream into a reality. Their level of financial success and professional recognition is such that it places them at the very pinnacle of their profession, indeed, these are the superstars of the speaking world." In choosing these top professionals Jeffreys wrote that his criteria included that the professionals must be full-time speakers, they had to have one book published, and be ranked by the Fortune 500 companies and major trade associations. They had to be financially successful and have earned at least $1 million a year. In interviewing the speakers, he found that several earned tens of millions of dollars annually from their speaking engagements and product sales. Keep in mind that this book was written in 1996. But these professional speakers were at the top of their profession. I wanted to introduce you to motivational speakers that could present to you alternative ways of becoming successful. Some may use the words Law of Attraction in their presentations and some may never. But each of their personae speaks of Success, finding your purpose in life and becoming that person you want to be. Jeffrey's book, was primarily written with a slant toward understanding how to be a successful professional speaker. But I offer some of their secrets of success because they adhere to the Laws of Attraction.

There are multiple ways of receiving the benefits of motivational speakers including, purchasing new and used books, and audio and video recordings. You can also borrow these items from your public library.

Jeffery's first successful speaker is **Anthony Robbins** and, he explains, in high school, in 1978, he was only 5'10" tall when one of his teachers informed him that he would be an excellent public speaker. From that point on Robbins concentrated on becoming the best speaker, he could be. Demanding excellence for himself and giving his audience more than they expected. At the time of Jeffreys' writing, in 1996, Robbins had grown from 5 feet 10 inches in high school to 6 feet 7 inches and a commanding presence. Through books, personal appearances and recorded training programs Robbins has earned millions. Early in his career, his audio tapes of his Personal Power presentation brought in $180 million in sales. His presentations have included as many as 5000 guests. Robbins presentations are so dynamic and the guests so excited that at the end all the attendees follow him across a bed of burning hot coals unharmed.

Jeffreys summarizes his writings on Robbins with eighteen of **Robbins'** success secrets. They summarize briefly how to be a successful professional speaker. But two of them I include here pertain to our discussions on the Law of Attraction and success. Number one- "Put your dreams, goals, and desires in writing." Number two- "the key to achieving your goals is that you must make them a "have to," a "gotta have it," and a "can't live without it." (Attitude)

Next Jeffreys offers **Dr. Wayne W Dyers'** secrets of success, they are; "Believing in your own ideas, abilities, and decision-making ability is a first step to achieving success in life," "that which you think about expands therefore, develop the habit of always focusing on what you want, not on what you don't want," "True inner peace will always elude you until you get your life "on purpose," "When pursuing a goal, the most important thing is to continually hold in your mind the picture of yourself successfully achieving that goal." "The clearer you see a goal in your mind, the easier it is to know what action you need to take to achieve that goal," "In order to achieve your vision you must be self-reliant; if you cannot find the circumstances that you need, then you must go out and create them," "When it comes to pursuing your life's purpose, giving up is not an option," "The way you conquer a fear is by facing it head-on," "When you stop focusing on money, and you get your life "on purpose," the money will come,"

Barbara De Angellis' shared this secret; "Getting quiet and tuning in to the silence within you will put you in touch with your highest self–the knower within you– the essence of who you really are."

Brian Tracy's secrets are; "By reading books, listening to audio tapes, (and video DVD), and attending seminars, you can learn, a few hours, the knowledge that has taken successful men and women years to acquire." "Successful people are intensely action-oriented." "How you view the world plays a key role in how successful you will be." "Life is a cause– and– affect process; whatever causes you initiate, you will reap the effects." "Positive people have simply made thinking in a positive way a habit."

Mark Victor Hansen's success secrets are; "Remember that (Jack Canfield's) Chicken Soup for the Sole was rejected 10 times before it was finally picked up. It may take 10 or 20 or 50 tries, but if you believe in your idea and don't give up, eventually you will succeed." Note; (Chicken Soup for the Soul book series has sold over 110 million copies in the United States and Canada.)

A success secret from **Roger Dawson** is; "Success is a habit- the more success you have the easier achieving success becomes."

Tom Hopkins success secrets are; "Whatever you want in life has a price. Decide to pay that price quickly and energetically. That way, while others are still paying off their debt, you'll be busy reaping the rewards of your effort." "Your enthusiasm acts like a powerful magnet to draw people in and make them want to listen to your message. Like the American Express card, you should never give a presentation without it." "If you constantly think of ways you can do more for your customer this week than you did last week, you will soon leave your competition in the dust." "Is what you're doing on a daily basis getting you closer to the things that you say are important to you in life?" **Jack Canfield's** Philosophy for Life; "I believe there is a God. I believe that we can each tune into inner guidance from God, whether you call it tuning in to your higher self or praying to Jesus, or whatever particular religious belief structure is. When you do this, your life is in a sense guided by the deepest part of yourself which is in tune with the external flow of the universe. And then the question is, "Do you trust yourself to trust that voice and take action on it?" When people love and accept themselves fully, they do that. I believe that if everyone did what they truly in their heart believed, then the whole world would work." **Joel Weldon's** success secrets are; "Integrity is good for business." "Promise a lot and then deliver more." "Success starts with a solid foundation." **Danielle Kennedy's** success secrets are; "Personal growth never stops: You want to constantly develop and hone your skills and all aspects of your life right up until the day the good Lord called your number!" "By making a name for yourself in one industry, that will often give you the credibility necessary to get work in other industries." "The real value of having money is that it allows you to buy time- time to do the things you love." "Having a mentor can often take years off your learning curve. Because they've "been there," they can give you invaluable advice and support." "From gratitude comes abundance. No abundance or prosperity can come into our house without a grateful heart." **Mike Ferry's** success secrets are; "Be sure you know and can clearly communicate to others the purpose of your business and the services it provides." **Art Linkletter's** success secrets are; "Being able to forget about yourself and become genuinely interested in other people is the key to success in sales, and speaking and in life." "The best people to interview are those over 70 and under 10, because they say exactly what they think!" "When you get burned in business, you can either sit around smoldering about it or you can do what all successful men and women do: use the experience as a catalyst to fire you up to achieve something even greater." "You know speaking is your passion if the time you feel most alive is when you are in front of an audience, motivating, educating, stimulating, and leaving behind something good in people's hearts and minds." "If you want to become rich and successful, develop relationships with rich and successful people!" "Success comes from doing what you love. What good would it be if at the end of your life you have money and fame, but you achieved it doing something you didn't like for all those years?" **Patricia Fripps'** success secrets are; "If you aspire to be one of the best in your field, ask yourself every day,

"How can I do this better?" "The most important element in building your business is keeping in touch with your customers." "You develop the confidence to face a new goal by remembering previous successes you've had in the past and saying to yourself, "Since I've done these other things, there's no reason why I can't be successful at this new goal." "Rather than focusing on money, work on becoming the kind of person people like to do business with, and the money will follow." **Leo Buscaglia's** success secrets are; "Never compare yourself to anyone else. You are unique! And what you have to contribute is special and different than what somebody else has to contribute." "Learning to really pay attention to the people and events in your life will make you a better communicator." "The only bad experiences are the ones you don't learn from" "Once you not only understand, but also joyfully except the fact that human beings (and that includes yourself!) are not perfect, life just seems to run a lot smoother." "The first step to being creative is believing that you are creative." "You know you've achieved a certain level of growth when you can genuinely respect other people and their feelings, even if they differ from your own." To change your life, find your purpose then find a way to make it happen. Napoleon Hill wanted to learn how to be successful. So, he interviewed hundreds of successful men and found the way. Whatever you want to do, whatever you want to be, can be accomplished. By learning these success secrets from successful people and by using the principles of the Law of Attraction, perseverance, dedication, visualization, and hard work you can accomplish all of your desires. A famous quote I heard years ago but never learned of the originator is "If you want to fly with Eagles, you must become an Eagle."

There is a story about a shoe manufacturer that wanted to expand their shoe sales into new areas. So, the sales manager talked with two of his top salespeople and explained they wanted to expand into an area where they have never sold shoes before. Both salespeople, excited about new opportunities, ventured into this unknown area to learn if they could sell shoes there. Sometime later, after both had the opportunity to survey this new territory, they returned to make their report to the sales manager. The first salesperson began with "Boss this area is absolutely terrible I can't sell any shoes in this area at all. Nobody wears shoes. I can't sell a thing." The second salesperson then spoke with the manager and, very excitedly, explained; "This is fantastic I have the greatest opportunity I have ever had in my life. Nobody wears shoes. This is the greatest sales area I have ever found. I cannot wait to get started selling shoes." There is opportunity where you find it. Attitude is one of your greatest assets. Use the Law of Attraction and create the opportunities you want. Surround yourself with beautiful people. Find your perfect purpose in life and build the life you want to lead.

Notes

96

What I Believe-Truth
Chapter 6
Esoteric

The definition of Esoteric is; something to be understood only by a group of special people or only those chosen. Even now adapts say truth will be revealed only to those who are ready to receive it. As we begin the chapter on Esoteric, I want to advise you of false psychics, charlatans, and palm readers. The ability of a person to have psychic abilities and clairvoyance, (which is stronger), is a gift from God. The people who have this gift understand it is a gift of God and can be taken away. They respect this gift and try to stay true to its value. When working with a psychic be wary of their predictions of the future or statements of the past until they have been proven to your satisfaction. One way to look at future predictions is that you must always know that every minute of every day you have choice and your path can change direction with the simple change in your thoughts. Think of a road map on which you are traveling to a certain destination and following one Highway but then you reach a junction where you could possibly turn in a different direction. That is, an example that might be used if a psychic tells you, you are going to make a long cruise across the ocean to a certain destination. That's fine as long as the ship's captain follows the same compass direction to arrive at its original destination. But think of your travel as tree branches of a large tree. The roadmap is a two-dimensional pathway whereas the tree branches are a three-dimensional pathway. As you travel along the tree branch in route to the destination the psychic gave you; you will come to multiple branches, which could be a desired change of thought, ultimately leading you to a different destination than what was proposed by the psychic. Always remember nothing is written in stone because we as humans have choice and we also must follow our path of Karma. This Law of attraction can become very complicated when you think how it is tied to other controlling effects within our lives. Over one hundred years ago, during the beginning of the religious new age/new thought movement, many leaders began to stand out in this movement to demonstrate and teach its principles. Two principles within the initial leadership of the church of The Theosophical Society, **Annie Besant**, 1847- 1933, and

Charles W. Leadbeater, 1854- 1934, wrote the book *"Thought- Forms."* With the help of several artists they presented artistic representations of the different moods of people they used as test subjects. In their book they explain that the many moods of people are represented in colors within the human aura. Thought forms within the aura can also be represented in different patterns. As an example of these colors, a bright red indicates anger, and flashes of a lurid red and dark brown indicate noble indignation. A clear brown shows avarice. A hard-dull brown gray can be a sign of selfishness. A deep heavy gray designates depression while a pale gray designates a sense of fear. A gray green is a signal of deceit and yet a brownish green with points and flashes of scarlet shows jealousy. I leave this explanation of colors within the aura as it is now. Further study can be attained by reading the book Thought-Forms.

Even more complicated within the human aura is the Akashic record of the individual. This record, as taught by the Theosophists, contains the total past thoughts, events, and emotions of the individual. It is believed, by Theosophists, that a high-minded spiritual clairvoyant or psychic can read this past record of an individual. This subject is too complicated to be discussed in this writing except to say how important events of the past life can play on an individual in the present life. I introduce this latest information about the aura simply to show that past lives affect one's present life.

Life Before Birth- From the teachings of the Theosophical Society I now present the following; We, as believers of the Christian teachings (New Age, metaphysical) believe that the human consists of three parts, the mortal physical body, the spiritual body, and the eternal soul. We believe that when a person dies the physical body stops operating and the spiritual body and the soul leave that physical body. I tend to believe the teachings of the Theosophists which say that the spirit is then on the astral (spiritual) plane, a different dimension, what some people would call heaven. I believe that this spiritual plane consists of what you would call Angels or what we of the new age movement call Spirit Guides or "Guardian Angels." It is at this time, in which the person is somewhat lost and confused but will soon become accustomed to this spiritual plane through the help of Spirit Guides and past loved ones. While on this plane of existence, the spirit is learning and doing things they must learn and prepare for the next life. I believe part of that responsibility is to be a guardian angel or a helper for a mortal. Part of the spirits learning on the astral plane is to learn from past mistakes. For example, if within the last lifetime the person never learned compassion then the spirit, on this plane, is to learn compassion and display this in the next life. During each lifetime, due to the Law of Attraction, we attract to us positive and negative Karma. As we attract negative Karma it tends to build up and become burdensome. This negative karma attracts negativity to us, meaning bad luck. Bad things seem to happen in our life. Our positive thoughts create positive karma. Our negative thoughts create negative karma. The only way we get rid of this negative Karma is through positive events. The more positive loving events we experience the more we eliminate negative Karma. As we move from lifetime to lifetime, we create both negative and positive karma, and hopefully, we learn to create more positive Karma. On the astral plane, the spirit receives the lessons they must learn in the next life. Then, for the spirit to accomplish what he or she is supposed to, in the next life, they are allowed to choose their parents and the environment to which the spirit is to be born to in the next life. This Law of Attraction follows us from lifetime to lifetime and is part of our evolution. This is why it is so important that we monitor our thoughts. We must learn to control and eliminate any anger or depression or any other thoughts that are negative for they only do us harm. By always having a positive/loving outlook on life, we live properly within the Law of Attraction. While we are on the subject of reincarnation and past lives I would like to discuss **Sylvia Browne's** book *"The Other Side And Back."* She was born with psychic abilities and as a child surprised many with her comments and predictions. As a child she was confused about psychic happenings but, many of these events were explained to her by her grandmother who was also, a psychic. In chapter 5 of her book, *Life After Life: How To Discover Your Own Past Lives*, she explains how she was first introduced into the idea of past lives while her patients were under hypnosis during treatment. Through further investigations, and the approval of other associate doctors, she began the practice of providing past life regression sessions with her clients. Like Ruth Montgomery, in her investigations of past lives, she discovered more truths about our eternal life. While I believe that past life regressions can bring you more understanding about yourself, I must insist on being careful. In Sylvia Brown's case she was a qualified hypnotist and performed past life regressions safely. I personally do not believe in hypnotism because there are some unscrupulous people in this world. I had a past life regression with a master clairvoyant while only in a mild session of meditation. You may consider contacting a local psychic or clairvoyant who will help you with a past life regression session but I personally, would not recommend hypnotism unless you have a close friend present during the hypnotism to guarantee that it is done safely. To those readers who decide to have a past life regression session, like Sylvia Browne recommends, I recommend that if you are told in a past life you were a famous person like Caesar or George Washington or Abraham Lincoln or Mme. Curie, you might consider a second opinion.

In **Sylvia Brown's** books, *Life On The Other Side- A Psychics Tour Of The Afterlife*, and *The Other Side And Back- A Psychics Guide To Our World And Beyond*, she explains the true meanings of our everlasting life eternal. She explains about spirit guides and Angels and how she has reunited others with the spirits of their departed loved ones. And she explains how your spirit guides and Angels are around you all the time always being there trying to help you. Her books are about reincarnation and how if we truly learn we have had past lives and that we live forever then there is no death. We already have, through God's grace, eternal life here and now.

For those readers most interested in exploring the spirit world, the other side, I strongly recommend reading Sylvia Browne's books. All thought within the spirit world comes from the Universal Mind and at this point I must explain, or correct, some present thinking. Our Creator, our God, what I call the Divine Infinite Spirit does not reside in a place called heaven. It is not a physical place. Our Creator is on the Spiritual plane of existence. You and I are on this material plane called earth. But spiritually, we live, move, breathe, and have our being within the spirit of God. This Divine Infinite Spirit surrounds us completely. We are one with Spirit. When we meditate and go within our minds, we close out the physical world, we try to get in touch with this Universal Mind. Every morning when I meditate, I shut out the physical world, and I try to get in touch with the Divine Infinite Spirit. I acknowledge that I am grateful for all the many blessings that, Spirit has bestowed upon me. Being grateful is one of the most important things within the Law of Attraction. This is called the Law of Gratitude. I then thank Spirit for protection for myself and my family. I thank Spirit for forgiveness for all of my transgressions and I ask the Divine Infinite Spirit for guidance in all that I do. When I have a problem that needs clarification, I ask Spirit to open the Universal Mind so that I may seek proper guidance. Getting in touch with Spirit and the Universal Mind is so important when we are trying to solve a problem in our daily lives. Our mind is how we get in touch with our Creator, not through loud voices or falling prostrate on the ground, but quiet contemplation with the One. Everyone should have a quiet time to meditate, if only to plan their daily activities. Quiet solitude relieves stress from the busy hustle of life. To learn meditation the expensive way, you could contact **Craig Hamilton at The Great Integral Awakening at HTTP://www.greatintegralawakening.com/**. Craig Hamilton's meditation exercises are expensive, and can cost you several hundred dollars, but they are an excellent start on your journey of spiritual enlightenment. If you are a beginner I would recommend either a good book or a rather inexpensive audio CD, these will give you instructions on relaxing the mind and body to put you in the meditative state. Once in this quiet calm serenity you can begin to search the inner self in quiet contemplation for what you're looking for. Many people, who enjoy meditation, also use yoga exercises I personally do not. But once again, searching for enlightenment does not have to be your goal. You just might want this quiet time to organize your business plans for the coming day and this will relieve stress. Getting in touch with the universal mind, through meditation, can also mean getting in touch with spirit beings on the spirit plane. These messages that we receive during contemplation come to us, usually, in the form of ideas. They may come to you by hearing a voice within your own mind. This voice that you might hear should be your own voice like when you are reading a book or magazine and pronouncing the words in your own mind. Just remain calm and listen for your spirit guide. If you sense nothing new, just close calmly and tell spirit thank you for all the blessings in your life, for protection from all harm, for forgiveness for your transgressions and thank you for guidance in all you do.

In the writings of the new age/new thought movement of the 1800's through those of the present 21st century, writers have spoken of a New Age of Enlightenment when the world is entering into the age of Aquarius, a new age when mankind should reach a higher understanding of their association with the creator and how we relate to all life in the universe. In **Ruth Montgomery's** book, *The World to Come – The Guides Long-Awaited Predictions for the Dawning Age*, she writes that mankind is to experience a new self-awareness as we enter into a new millennia and a thousand years of peace and enlightenment. We will learn a stronger relationship between ourselves, nature, and spirit, our Creator. Earlier in these writings we discussed intuition. Physical scientists have no real explanation for intuition primarily because intuition comes mentally through the spirituality of the Universal Mind and its connectivity to the subconscious mind. Scientists are investigating all DNA and even have experimented with changing DNA for a desired result, such as eliminating all flu viruses. But DNA is programmed through evolution and Mother Nature. I read one article recently that a scientist was investigating the abilities of telepathy and said that telepathy must be the action of electrons carrying information through space from one individual to another individual. I personally would challenge that idea since I believe that electrons are on the physical/ material plane and not on the spiritual plane. I believe there is a thin veil of understanding between intuition, DNA, and electrons. In other words, between understanding the difference between the physical and the spiritual. **Madam Blavatsky**, in *The Secret Doctrine,* called this the Veil of Isis.

Now, in keeping with the idea of a new self-awareness and the age of Enlightenment, I would like to express the ideas in **Ken Carey's** book *The Third Millennium- Living In The Post Historic World*. In chapter 7, entitled The Spontaneous Precision of Instinct, Carey discusses intuition and instinct. He writes; "The information that enters your awareness is subject to interpretation by two separate yet potentially (and prehistorically) compatible systems. The system designed to be your primary system functions autonomically below the level of conscious awareness. In that system information is organized and interpreted by the spirit. In the system designed initially to be your backup or supplemental system, information is organized and interpreted by subjective associations. This system, of course, is the one with which you are historically most familiar." The problem that has arisen is we have forgotten this connection between spirit and the subjective mind. Carey continues to write, in a section called Living Instinctually; "In the historical condition, instinctual input is ignored. The cultures that dominate human values mistrusts so deeply, in fact, the children are taught from their earliest years to fear their instincts. Young people intuitively sense that without help their egos are incapable of effectively managing their affairs, and culture plays upon this sense. It distorts the truth behind this insight by teaching each new generation that since their egos are inadequate, they must develop a social persona, a protective veneer, an image of themselves behind which they can retreat in safety, forever after pursuing physical-plane relationships from behind a mask. Occasionally, overtly, but more often through 1000 forms of subliminal persuasion issuing from virtually every culturally adjusted person they encounter; the young are taught that the development of a self–image is an urgent matter of grave importance. The sense of self that cultured children subsequently adapt is

superficial and fictitious." "To live spontaneously, instinctually; To simply be. To say the right words without thinking them out ahead of time. To experience the purity of the mind uncluttered by troublesome and misplaced responsibility. To know exactly the right gesture, the right behavior, the creative response for each and every situation. Such are the birthrights of each and every human being. Every child comes into the world with his or her instinctual awareness healthy and intact. In the coming civilizations of the stars, children will mature not only retaining this ability but developing it, honing it to a fine art. They and their societies will live instinctually from moment to moment, as you are now invited to begin living. Trust yourself, your instincts, your intuitive senses. Except the birthright that has unfolded with you from out of the Being behind all being. When you receive God, you receive the consciousness that precedes all manifestation, the limitless consciousness of eternal love that was from the beginning is now, and ever shall be before, beyond, above, and within all relationship. This consciousness is the greatest gift that anyone could ever receive."
Ken Carey- *The Third Millennium- Living In*

The Post-historic World. In Ruth Montgomery's writings, her spirit channeler's explained that the purpose of all this information presented to us is to help us to remember and truly understand that there is no such thing as death. Life is eternal. We simply travel from the material plane to the spiritual plane, and when we are ready, we create and enter a new material form to continue our journey of evolution.

Ken Carey writes, in his book, ***The Third Millennium,*** "There is but the finest veil between you and a full dimensional perception of reality, the filmiest of screens between you and your eternal self. You require no elaborate technique or ritual to release this veil. You need only open to the organic current of awareness that in every moment flows to you from the source of all life." This Veil of Isis, as it is called, is what blocks us from the truth that we are true spiritual beings. In the writings of Ken Carey, Ruth Montgomery, and Helena P. Blavatsky they explain that the true meaning of the Holy Bible's explanation of the expulsion of the original Adam and Eve from the garden of Eden (Eden is a metaphor- not a real place- but a story) is explained this way; it was the original thought/idea that mankind would create a material body to be temporarily occupied by the spiritual being. That spirit would enjoy this beautiful bounty of mother nature and still spend half of the linear time on the spiritual plane. That is, half of the time on the spiritual plane and the other half on the material plane. But mankind became so enamored while enjoying the five physical senses of the human form they forgot to return to the spiritual plane. Therefore with successive incarnations in human form we developed a Veil of Isis. This is how today we have forgotten who we really are and this explains mankind's fall from grace.

Montgomery explains, in her books, that the Creator has been sending highly advanced Spirits to assist us in remembering our true identity. Some of these highly Enlightened Spirits have become walk-ins in human form and others have remained on the spiritual plane impressing their knowledge on humankind through meditation and atonement.

We now enter into a discussion of spirit Walk-ins in which highly enlightened individuals are here now as leaders to help guide us through these turbulent times to a better place of understanding ourselves.

The writings of **Ruth Montgomery's** book

"Strangers Among Us" explains this idea of Walk-ins. She explains at the beginning of chapter 1, "There are Walk-ins on this planet. Tens of thousands of them. Enlightened beings, who, after successfully completing numerous incarnations, have attained sufficient awareness of the meaning of life that they can forgo the time-consuming process of birth and childhood, returning directly to adult bodies. A Walk-in is a, spiritually, high-minded entity who is permitted to take over the body of another human being who wishes to depart. Since a Walk-in must never enter a body without the permission of its owner this is not to be confused with those well publicized cases (such as were described in (The Three Faces of Eve, The Exorcist, et al) in which multiple egos or evil spirits are vying for possession of an inhabited body. The motivation for a walk-in is humanitarian. He returns to physical being in order to help others help themselves, planting seed-concepts that will grow and flourish for the benefit of mankind.

Some of the world's greatest spiritual and political leaders, scientist, and philosophers in ages past are said to have been Walk-ins, but in these final decades of the 20th century the pace has been steadily accelerating, and many more of them are entering mature physical bodies to prepare us for the shift of the earth on its axis at the end of the century, and the New Age that is donning. Not all Walk-Ins are towering leaders. Many are working quietly among us today, going about their unsung task of helping us to understand ourselves, to seek inner guidance, and to develop a philosophy that will sustain us through the trying times ahead. You may know a Walk-in in your own office or in your community. They seldom reveal themselves, because to do so would imperil the good work for which they were returned to physical being. In fact, you yourself may be a Walk-in! Since the memory pattern of the departing entity survives intact, Walk-ins are sometimes unaware of their altered status for several years after the substitution has been affected." Before Montgomery started writing this new book on walk-ins, she explained she did not have any new ideas for providing a book when she received a letter from an unknown correspondent who mentioned she was disappointed in not having a new book to read. So, she then suggested that Montgomery consult her spirit guides and ask about the role of Walk-Ins on this planet. The correspondent then explained to Montgomery;

"a Walk-in is a highly evolved entity who, always with permission, enters the body of a human who wishes to check out before completing the tasks, he has begun. Sometimes a human has lost heart, or had taken on a task more difficult than he was prepared to handle. Sometimes it was the purpose of the departing human to begin the task and prepare the body for the new entity. The Walk-in first completes the tasks of the body's previous owner, and then goes on to do what he must do on his own projects, which are really those of a gardener who plants seeds on the planet, helps those seeds to germinate, and then lets them grow in their own direction. If you ask, your unseen friends will tell you more. They will also mention political, military, spiritual, and philosophical leaders, who were walk-ins, who inspired or led people, and who are remembered for what they started. Perhaps it is time to tell the story of these remarkable beings, who are human while they are among us and who help us along the way in our own evolution." After consulting with her spirit guides Montgomery continues "in past centuries Walk-ins have flowered and waned and come again, and they are a prime example of the immortality of the soul. Thus, those who attain to a sufficiently advanced level need not repeat the learning process of birth, babyhood, and schooling in order to serve others. By electing to enter directly into an adult body no longer wanted by the occupant, they bring with them a deepened awareness, a fresher recollection of the Akashic records and goals to be reached, and are able to communicate personally, with other earthlings, unlike the spirit entities who are ever present but seldom seen or heard by those in physical body." With further research on Walk-ins the spirit guides explained "living Walk-ins should not be publicly identified while still in flesh, because to do so would hamper the purpose of their return to earthly being. They do not need ego trips! They come, not as masters or authorities, but as servants and workers whose task it is to help others discover Truth for themselves." She further writes "By contrast, the Guides readily agreed to name some other Walk-ins, because they are not presently incarnate. Among them are: Mohandas K. Gandhi (1869- 1948)," who rallied a slumbering giant [India] to action without benefit of sort, thereby freeing that nation." Benjamin Franklin (1706 – 1790), the printer, author, publisher, inventor, scientist, public servant, and diplomat, who has been called the first civilized American, and America's first world statesman. Abraham Lincoln (1809 – 1865), taking over from a country lawyer, "who after several traumatic experiences and violent headaches withdrew in favor of the lofty entity who entered that body, signed the Emancipation Proclamation, and sadly, led America into a divisiveness but necessary war to free the countless souls rapped in slavery." Harvey Firestone (1868 – 1938), who virtually put the modern world on wheels by pioneering the manufacture of pneumatic and balloon tires. Emmanuel Swedenborg (1688 – 1772), who, after having attained the highest pinnacle of scientific "fame" and propounding all that the world was prepared to understand or conceive at that time, willingly gave up earthly fame and fortune to step aside, so that a transcendental soul might use that well body to teach the oneness of the spiritual and physical world. The Guides say the new entity arrived after the experience in which the original entity (the scientist) saw the heavens opened wide, and realized that his own work was satisfactorily completed and that another would further the cause of mankind by taking over his physical body. "A prime example of the good that comes from Walk-ins arriving fully armed for their work as   adults," the guides added." Joseph, the Biblical Canaan lad with the coat of many colors, who, after being sold into slavery by jealous brothers, stepped aside for a highly evolved entity who interpreted the dreams of the Pharaoh, and rose to become a wise governor of Egypt. The Christ Spirit, who according to the Guides, became the greatest of the Walk-ins" at the time of the Nazarene's baptism when God became manifest in the man Jesus. "The Guides will have more to say about this later, but it is interesting to note that Edgar Casey, the seer of Virginia Beach, also said that the Christ Spirit did not enter until Jesus was baptized by John the Baptist." While we are on the subject of Jesus, the Nazarene and the Christ, I would like to delve into his life. We have received a great deal of Esoteric information from the book titled, *True Esoteric Traditions* by **M. Dale Palmer**. This book was written by a Rosicrucian and contains many of the Rosicrucian religious beliefs. While Ruth Montgomery explains in her books that Jesus received the Christ Spirit when he was baptized by John the Baptist, Dale Palmer writes that the baptism of Jesus, by John the Baptist, was only a reenactment since Jesus had been baptized several times earlier in other cultures. Since Jesus received the Christ Spirit, most likely, sometime after his childhood we can speculate that he had a quite normal childhood. Ruth Montgomery wrote In Her Book **Companions along the Way**, that in one of her past lives she had been the sister of Lazarus and her name at that time was also, Ruth. She mentions that Lazarus and Jesus were best friends as children and played together often. According to information I have read in the past, Jesus was born in the year 3 BC but, according to Dale Palmer he believes Jesus was born on May 29, 7 BC. According to Jewish tradition at the time; for 4000 years Jews had been expecting a Messiah and that date was the date of zero exactly between BC and DC on their calendar. But when Jesus arrived, somewhere between 7 BC and 3 BC, he was not accepted as their Messiah possibly because Jesus was not born unto a Hebrew family. Jesus' parents, Joseph and Mary, were members of the Essene Jewish sect and not of the Hebrew race and here we have to explain a point of contention in the birth of Jesus. **Dale Palmer** wrote in his book, **True Esoteric Traditions**, that the Essene sect initially were very strict, so much so that, they believed in celibacy. But then, they realized that if they wanted the sect to continue, they had to reconsider celibacy. So, they set up strict guidelines for members. When young men and women decided they wanted to marry they were allowed to become betrothed. But that betrothal had strict guidelines. They were allowed to become betrothed/engaged for a period of three years at which time they were allowed to be married within the church. But, during that betrothal period of three years, intimacy was not allowed. But, young people, being what they are, sometimes could not resist. Many young couples including Joseph and Mary had intimacy henceforth the child Jesus. So, the Essene's declared these births holy and in the case of Mary, as the Bible states, had an Immaculate Conception. Also, another point of contention was that Joseph, and his son Jesus, were heirs to the throne of King David. The problem here is there was 1000 years between the reign of King David and the birth of Jesus. 1000 years of multiple generations does not allow very much of a birthright to a throne.

In his book Palmer explains that the Essene's believed in education and sometime before Jesus was five years of age the family was visited by three wise men to arrange Jesus' education. When he reached age 5 Jesus attended school, it is believed in the eastern Mediterranean area. Jesus' whereabouts from age 12 to the age of 30 are somewhat unknown but it is believed he studied many religions including Buddhism during this time period and attended the secret schools called the White and Blue Lodges. Both of these Lodges have been hidden and secretive for thousands of years. Even today it is difficult to learn of them but there will come a time in the near future when their secrets will be available to all that desire their teachings. Truths cannot be hidden forever. It's been written that Emperor Constantine, who had been a Pagan all his life, was allowed to learn the teachings of the White Lodge, but not the Blue Lodge, and that, upon his deathbed, he accepted the Christian religion. In the Holy Bible Jesus disciples called him Master or Master Jesus. Palmer writes that this comes from a ritual that Jesus performed during his early training. Supposedly, deep within the Great Pyramid of Giza, there is a pit. (Note; James Churchward's book *The Lost Continent of Mu* chapter XVI; Accent Sacred Mysteries, Rites and Ceremonies, explains the rituals of the ancient Egyptians. Also, page 325 depicts a drawing of the great pyramid in Egypt showing a chamber and its entrances deep within the pyramid.) A secret ritual of the Freemasons was to allow an initiate to spend three days within this secret chamber having absolute darkness and very little, if any, oxygen. During this time the Initiate must control his mind and shut down his body, slowing down his breathing and his heart rate to almost nothing thereby protecting himself from the extreme surroundings. Those initiates that failed to do this either died or went insane. This was strictly voluntary. Like a bear that hibernates for months during the winter or when a frog living in a small pond experiences a drought of months with a hot summer, and the water disappears, the frog buries himself in the mud and completely shuts down his bodily processes and survives this time of drought until the water returns to the pond and he emerges. So, the initiate in the deep bowels of the great pyramid totally shuts down his bodily functions supposedly to release the idea of the ego. It's been said that many of the students did not survive this ritual. It is believed that Aristocles, Plato, and Jesus performed this ritual. When the initiate attained the mastery of this procedure, they were considered a Master. Hence, Jesus attained the name of Master Jesus It is not known when Master Jesus accepted the Christ Spirit but it is well accepted that when he was known as Jesus Christ he was the most perfect human to walk the face of this earth. But we must understand that anyone can receive the Christ Spirit. Many religions and writers do not accept that Master Jesus Christ was God incarnate, nor that Jesus was the only Son of God. The material body known as Jesus accepted a highly advanced spirit, an highly Enlightened being with the Christ Spirit to bring the message of eternal life to humankind at a highly contentious time on earth, that message being that we already have eternal life we have only to learn how to recognize it.

Montgomery continues; "My spirit friends say that since a Walk-in automatically inherits the memories of the departing entity, he may continue for some time to identify himself with the John or Mary Dough he has replaced, but he will immediately begin to discover within himself a new awareness of life energies, deeper perceptions, clearer goals, and a love for all beings. The often-muddled individual who vacated the body is replaced by one who intuitively knows how to solve the problems that blocked the others progress. The Walk-in for a time may believe that he has simply been granted new insight, and because he has agreed, before entering the body, to complete the task begun by the Walkout, few of his associates will suspect the substitution of egos. Yet as time passes, and the person becomes more energetic, hopeful, and dedicated, relatives and friends will remark on the great improvement in his attitude. Passivity is gone, and with it the previous reluctance to attack new problems and find a way out of the despair or boredom. When such improvement occurs associates at first will marvel at the alteration but then will come to accept that the person has successfully passed through a period of depression."

For those who wish to do further investigation on Walk-ins I strongly suggest purchasing and reading **Ruth Montgomery's** book *Strangers Among Us.*

To further investigate the spiritual Esoteric, I include **Ken Carey's book *"Starseed Transmissions"* he opens his writing this way**; "The communications that I present in this book seem to have been transmitted neurobiologically. As I communed with these spatial intelligences, our bio gravitational fields seemed to merge, our awareness's blended, and my nervous system seemed to become available to them as a channel for communication. At times I considered these extraterrestrial, at other times, angelic. Occasionally, I thought of the entities as informational cells within a Galactic organism of some sort." For emphasis I repeat myself; in the writings of both Ruth Montgomery and Ken Carey, under the directions of the spirit beings, they write that we as humans have forgotten our origin and our true place within the spirit of the Creator. This is the meaning of the phrase "fall from grace," and the expulsion of Adam and Eve from the garden of Eden. As I see it, God, the Creator, created Spirit or sparks of energy and this energy was allowed to identify individually as ego. At this time the earth was already formed and contained animal and plant life and the spirits with ego were allowed to enter the bodies of the animals and plant life. These spirits enjoyed the physical forms of the animals and plant life and eventually were allowed to create and move into the physical form of humans. During this beginning time of spirits in physical form they were meant to be only half the time in physical form and the other half totally in the spiritual form. But now begins this so-called fall from grace. Spirits became so enamored with the physical form and the five physical senses which allows us to enjoy this beautiful playground called earth that they began to forget their spiritual origin. This is what is called the original Sin. We, mankind, have forgotten our spiritual connection to our Creator.

In **Ken Carey's** book The ***Starseed Transmissions***, the spirit announces that he finds Ken Carey's physical senses curious. The spirit says that we have a curious language of commerce and informs us that the best language to communicate with spirit is the language of Light. Note; (there are books available on this language of Light.) In one section of Ken Carey's book he tells us when God created spirits some were allowed to create egos and others were only to remain in spirit form as helpers and guardian angels to those spirits in physical form. So, I find it curious that spirit beings who give us instructions on what we as humans have forgotten about the true nature of God and the spirit world have never experienced the five physical senses of the human form. They have never experienced that soft summer breeze across your face and through your hair. Or seen, with physical eyes, the beauty of a lush forest, river, a beautiful waterfall and a beautiful young deer grazing in the sunlight. They have never seen, through physical eyes, the beauty of a newborn child or heard, through physical hearing, the soft cooing of that infant child. God, our Creator, has given us the power of choice and this beautiful playground we call earth to live on and when we understand this Law of Attraction, we can build ourselves a beautiful heaven on earth. I choose to be here now.

We must also understand and appreciate that Mother Nature's plants and animals contain spirits.

In **Jeremy Narby's** book, *Intelligence In Nature– An Inquiry Into Knowledge,* he writes how he searched in the Peruvian Amazon jungle to learn of the intelligence of nature. He searched for native Shaman and inquired about this intelligence. He writes; "Shamanism is transforming itself." "I caught a plane to Iquitos, the largest town in the Peruvian Amazon. From there I made my way to Zungarococha, Lake Catfish, to visit a teacher's training program at a bilingual, intercultural school, where young people from 15 indigenous societies learn to teach their own language and culture, as well as Spanish and science. I had an appointment with three "indigenous specialists"– men with extensive knowledge about their own language and culture, and teach at the training program. As these indigenous specialists work hand-in-hand with Peruvian professionals, such as mathematicians, linguists, and agronomists, they are used to relating indigenous knowledge to science. We met on the veranda of their living quarters, a small wooden house with mosquito screens overlooking the lake. They knew I wanted to interview them about intelligence in nature." The first specialist, Nahwari Rafael Chanchari, represented the Shawi people." "He dressed simply, wearing a short sleeve shirt, pants, and sandals. I started by asking him why he thought scientists had difficulty seeing the spirit side of the nature world. "Look," he replied, "I believe that science is materialistic. Science wants to see concrete evidence when it tries to answer the questions it asks itself. In the indigenous world, we also believe in the material. Trees exists, as matter, as wood, as firewood. But this material existence is not all there is to it. Deep down, they are also beings. And science recognizes this when it calls insects and trees living beings. We Shawi think that all living beings have souls, which have their own spirits. If they do not, they would not have a reason to live. Take a stone, for example. For science, a stone is organic matter, that is what I think they call it, matter which has no life. And it considers earth and water in the same way, as lacking life. But for the Shawi, a stone has its own soul, as does water. And earth also has its mother. For us, everything is alive." "Does each little stone have a soul?" "I asked." "It depends on the size. A simple little stone does not. But a stone which is ten square meters, or huge rocks which are 15 square meters, have mothers. Tiny little grains of sand do not. But when you go to the beach, you find that all the sand taken together, as a beach, has a mother, or a soul."

"He spoke Spanish fluently and appeared to have thought about these questions before. I asked if he could explain the difference between the "spirit" of an individual plant and its "mother." "He remained silent for an instant, then replied: "A tree has a soul like a human being does. The Christian world considers that humans have souls. It is the same with the tree. It is material and it also has a soul or a spirit which may present itself to you in your dreams in the form of a person. And taken together, trees have their mother, meaning to say, mother of the forest, and mother of the species. This is what we call tanaashi, mother of an ecosystem so to speak. For example, in a place where there are a lot of Irapay palms, that is where the mother of irapay lies. It is like a general soul. That is the difference between the mother and the soul of each tree."

Shamans use drugs or narcotics to investigate nature whereas scientists study nature through the physical sciences. That is why Science may never fully understand the metaphysical because they do not search for answers while using the nonphysical tools. During his research Narby spoke with Usi Kamarambi and inquired about his understanding about nature spirits. Narby writes; "he spoke basic Spanish with a thick, throaty accent. He went on to say that," "Kandoshi people use ayahuasca, datura (a narcotic) and tobacco to attain visions that allow them to understand nature." "He said he had used these plants himself and had spoken with the mothers of plants, in particular with the "owners of all species."

"I do not speak with the owner of animals, no. I could only see her. I could see where all the animals exist, many kinds of different animals. And there was their owner, the mother of animals." "He used the concepts of "owner" and "mother interchangeably." "What did she look like?" "I asked." "Her body was covered in feathers, feathers of animals, birds, and her feet were like a person's, and so were her fingers, but she had very long nails."

"He described the owner of animals as a hybrid being, as do many indigenous people around the world." "I steered the conversation toward the subject of intelligence in nature. I asked the specialist if they thought animals think. Akushi Butuna Karijuna, the Kichwa specialist, said," "We see animals, they have thought. Ants, for example, prepare their supplies, stock their food, go to fetch it, and bring it back to the right place." "Are they thinking about the future? I asked." "Thinking about the future," "he agreed." "That's why we, in our knowledge, say that animals also think. They know how they are going to save themselves, how they are going to prepare their nests."

To some readers the ideas in these writings are completely new and unnerving. This new thought can be easily accepted or rejected according to the readers past understandings and if they would continue to investigate other media, for this new thought, they may become satisfied.

I continue now with an extreme possibility on the beginnings of life on this earth that has been mentioned in several of my readings in the past.

Today, scientists have wondered why a large amount of animal life, including humans, have frog DNA in their own DNA. **Ruth Montgomery**, in the book, *"The World to Come"*, writes about the beginning of physical life on the earth. She writes; "There was a time when all humans were consolidated in one energy, which many of us call God. We were all one. Then the mighty mass began to emit sparks, and each was separated from the others. All felt the oneness, but also the desire for exploration as separate entities, and as the earth became populated by the lower species that we have mentioned, many of the sparks began to inhabit the bodies of animals, birds, fish, trees, and all living things. It was mystical and exciting, and for millennia the sparks or fragments of the Godhead continued to experiment, withdrawing from some life forms and entering others, to experience the novelty of life form. Some became so entangled in those forms that they refused to leave them, while others inspected, experienced, and moved on. Many stayed aloof from such physical manifestations, and soon became what you would call angels, unrestrained by physical form and free to observe and assist others. This, then, was the beginning of souls, and as the species evolved, some became higher than others in mental and spiritual development. Then came the creation of the human form for those of higher development." On other spirits not in physical form, she continues; "Since they (her spirit channelers) had mentioned angels in that discourse, I asked them to elaborate, and they declared: "As we have told you, angels are spirits who have not been born into flesh, but are filled with love and eager to help those in need. Everyone who is a believer in "God's will" attracts guardian angels and there are many types of angels in various stages of development, just as there are humans on earth and elsewhere." I (Montgomery) asked if they are able to see angels, and they continued: "we do see angels, but they are not as worldly ones depict them. They are radiant beings not of human form but who busy themselves with helpful acts of mercy or love. They indeed can assume human form when a sudden danger imperils an earthling who is worth rescuing through warnings or helpful acts, but in their normal state they assume no particular form. They were not born into earthly bodies, preferring to remain in the spirit realm and avoid the errors that we humans commit in earthly bodies. No, they don't have wings or harps. They move with their thoughts, just as we do in this stage of spirit being."

Montgomery continues;" It was intriguing to review the guides description of creation from a "void, a nothing, and an everything," but what, then, is God? Is He a force or a personal being to whom we can pray and from whom we can expect help? I put the question in writing, and the guides replied: "God is everything. He is the creative force and the glue that holds the universe together. He is also a personal counselor, since a part of Him is in you and every living thing. God is all! If we follow the true dictates of our own conscious, the divine spark, we will not go wrong. God does hear prayers, including the ones that you pray for us in the spirit plane. Don't ever doubt it, Ruth. This is the essential truth that guides us all."

The End

Notes

What I Believe-Truth

Appendix A
Recommended authors and writings;
   I highly recommend that you, Dear Reader, select, purchase and read the best books for you to continue your journey of understanding the esoteric knowledge necessary to create your Heaven on Earth. Thank you for reading my book.

Sincerely,
Bruce D. Durst

Andrews, Shirley, Author- *Lemuria and Atlantis; Studying The Past To Survive The Future.*
Assarf, John- Contributor- *The Secret.*
Besant, Annie - 1847- 1933, Clairvoyant, Author- *Esoteric Christianity, Thought Forms.* Church elder- The Theosophical Society.
Beckwith, Michael Bernard- Contributor- *The Secret,* Author-*Spiritual Liberation-Fulfilling Your Soul's Potential*
Blavatsky, Helena - 1831- 1891, Clairvoyant, Author- *The Secret Doctrine, Isis Unveiled.*

Difficult to read because of many strange words including Hindu, Buddhism and other eastern religious terminology, but much esoteric information is presented. Founder The Theosophical Society.

Browne, Sylvia - 1936- 2013, Author- *Life On The Other Side, The Other Side And Back.*

Buscaglia, Leo- Motivational Speaker, The Fall Of Freddie The Leaf: A Story Of Life For All Ages, Living Loving & Learning, Love: What Life Is All About.

Byrne, Rhonda - Author-*The Secret*.

Brower, Lee- Contributor- *The Secret*.

Canfield, Jack - Motivational Speaker, Contributor- *The Secret*, Author- *Key To Living The Law of Attraction. - Chicken Soup for the Soul*. Multiple books, audio and video.

Carey, Ken - - 2017, Psychic, Spirit Channeler,
Author- *The Starseed Transmissions, Return Of The Bird Tribes, The Third Millennium, Vision, Terra Christa.*

Carnegie, Andrew- 1835- 1919, Scottish American, worked as telegrapher, railroad owner, expanded the American steel industry and became of the richest man in America. Author- *The Autobiography of Andrew*

Carnegie and His Essay The Gospel of Wealth.

Carnegie, Dale Harbison- 1888- 1955, American writer and lecturer and developer of self- improvement courses. His most famous book was *How to Win Friends and Influence People.*

Castaneda, Carlos - 1925- 1998, Author- *The Teachings of Don Juan: A Yaqui Way Of Knowledge. Metaphysical.*

Cayce, Edgar - 1877- 1945, Author- *Edgar Cayce On Prophecy.*

Chopra, Deepak - 1947- , *The Seven Spiritual Laws Of Success.*

Churchward, Col James- 1851- 1936, Author- *The Lost Continent of Mu*.

Churchward, Jack- Author- *Lifting The Veil On The Lost Continent Of Mu- The Motherland of Men.*

Collier, Robert- 1885- 1950, Text contributed to The Secret. Author- self-help/new thought, the practical psychology of abundance, desire, faith, visualization, confident action, and personal development, *The Secret of the Ages.*

Davis, Roy Eugene- 1931- Author- *Light On The Spiritual Path.*

Dawson, Roger- Motivational speaker, Author- *Secrets of Power Negotiating,*

Weekend Millionaire's Secrets to Investing in Real Estate, Sales Revelation.
De Angelis Ph D, Barbara- Motivational speaker- Author- *Are You The One For Me: Knowing Who's Right and Avoiding Who's Wrong, Soul Shifts: Transformative Wisdom for Creating a Life of Authentic Awakening, Emotional Freedom & Practical Spirituality.* Audio and Video recordings on self-improvement. Contributor- *The Secret.*

Demartini, Dr. John F.- Contributor- *The Secret*

Diamond, Marie- Contributor- *The Secret*

Dooley, Mike- Contributor- *The Secret*

Doyle, Bob- Contributor- *The Secret*

Dwoskin, Hale- Contributor- *The Secret*, Author- *The Sedona Method- Your Key to Lasting Happiness, Success, Peace and Emotional Wellbeing. Happiness is Free: And It's Easier Than You Think, Letting Go! Three Steps To Emotional Well-Being* (Live.)

Dyer, Dr, Wayne W.- 1940- 2015- Motivational Speaker- Author- Multiple books, *The Power of Intention-, Your Erroneous Zones-*, Audio and Video recordings on self-improvement.

Ferry, Mike- Motivational Speaker, Author-*How To Develop A Six-Figure Income In Real Estate*.

Flammarion, Nicolas Camille, Astronomer, author- multiple books.

Fripp, Patricia- Motivational Speaker, Author-*Make It So You Don't Have To Fake It.*

Goodman, Morris- Contributor- *The Secret*

Gray, Dr. John- Contributor- *The Secret*.

Haanel, Charles- 1866- 1949, Text contributed to *The Secret*.

Hagelin, Dr. John- Contributor- *The Secret*.

Hansen, Mark Victor- Motivational speaker, author- *The One Minute Millionaire, The Miracles In You.*

Harris, Bill- Contributor- *The Secret*.

Hill, Napoleon- 1883- 1970, Author- *The Law Of Success, Think And Grow Rich.*

Holmes, Ernest- 1887- 1960, Author- The *Science Of Mind*, Founder of the Church of Religious Science.

Hopkins, Tom- Motivational speaker, Author- How to Master the Art of Selling.

Johnson, Dr. Ben- Contributor- *The Secret*.

Judge, William Quan- 1851-1896, Co-founder The Theosophical Society.

Kennedy, Danielle- Motivational speaker, Author-*How To List and Sell Real Estate*.

Leadbeater, Charles W.- 1854- 1934, Author-

The Inner Life, Thought Forms, Man Visible Invisible, The Astral Plane. Church elder- The Theosophical Society.

Langemeir, Loral- Contributor- *The Secret*.

Linkletter, Art- 1912- 2010, Motivational Speaker, Author- *How To Be Like Walt (Disney,) Kids Say The Darndest Things*.

Montgomery, Ruth- 1912- 2001, Spirit Channeler, Author- *A Search For The Truth, Born To Heal, Here And Hereafter, A World Beyond, The World Before, Strangers Among Us, Threshold To Tomorrow, Companions Along The Way, Aliens Among Us, The World To Come, Herald Of The New Age. A Search For The Truth.*

Mulford, Prentice- 1834- 1891 Text contributed to The Secret, *Thoughts Are Things-* (The White Cross Library.)

Narby, Jeremy- 1959- , Author- *Intelligence In Nature- An Inquiry Into Knowledge.*

Nichols, Lisa- Contributor- *The Secret,* Author- *Abundance Now: Amplify Your Life & Achieve Prosperity Today*.

Nightingale, Earl- 1921- 1989, Exceptional writer and self-improvement public speaker. Author- *Lead The Field, The Strangest Secret*.

Olcott, Henry Steel- 1832- 1907

Proctor, Bob- Philosopher- Contributor- *The*

Secret.
Quimby, Phineas Parkhurst- 1802- 1866, *The Complete Writings-* by Ervin Seale.
Ray, James Arthur- Contributor- *The Secret.*
Robbins, Anthony- Motivational Speaker- Author- *Unlimited Power-*, multiple books, audio and video recordings on self-improvement.
Schovel Shinn, Florence - 1871- 1940, Author- *The Game Of Life And How to Play It, The Wisdom Of Florence Schovel Shinn.*
Shimoff, Marci- Contributor- *The Secret.* Coauthor- *Chicken Soup For The Woman's Soul, Chicken Soup For The Mother's Soul.*
Carol Swiedler- 1922- 2007, Author- *Letters From The Cosmos.*
Tracy, Brian- Motivational Speaker, author *Eat That Frog, No Excuses- The Power of Self- Discipline, The Psychology of Selling, Goals.*
Vitale, Dr. Joe- contributor- *The Secret.*
Waitley, Dr. Denis, Contributor- *The Secret.*
Walsch, Neale Donald- contributor- Author- *The Secret*, Author- *Conversations With God.* Multiple books- audio, video.
Wattles, Wallace D.- 1860- 1911- Author- *The Complete Collection of Wallace D. Wattles-The Science of Getting Rich- The Science of Being Great- The Science of*

Being Well-How to Get What You Want-The New Science of Living and Healing. **Weldon, Joel-** Motivational Speaker, Author- *Presentation Excellence: 25 Tricks, Tips & Techniques for Professional Speakers and Trainers, The Weldon Blueprint: A Personal Plan for Success.*
White Eagle Lodge- New Lands Retreat House/Temple, Hampshire, UK. Writings- *Morning Light, Spiritual Unfoldment 1, Spiritual Unfoldment 2, Spiritual Unfoldment 3, Spiritual Unfoldment 4.*
Wolf, Dr. Fred Alan- contributor- *The Secret*, Author- *Taking The Quantum Leap.*

The End

Notes

What I Believe-Truth

Copyright-2018
Updated-2019
Bruce D. Durst
In cooperation with
Cyber Writers Gallery

ISBN 978-0-578-62383-2

Bruce D. Durst, born in Tuscaloosa, Alabama, USA is a U.S. Marine veteran of the 1962 Cuban Missile Crisis and the Vietnam war. His career included U.S. Marine Aviation- Avionics maintenance (communications, navigation and identification equipment on jet fighters) and maintaining communications and computer systems for Honeywell, GTE Information Systems, Texas Instruments and Paradyne Corporation. He is a member of the American Legion, the Marine Corps League and the First Marine Air Wing Association- Vietnam Service and attends their functions regularly. He enjoys family, writing, golf, travel, and sportscar races.
His website is cyberwritersgallery.com and includes his writing and photography.

ISBN- 978-0-578-62383-2